1994.

BRITAIN AND
THE UNITED STATES

BRITAIN
AND THE
UNITED STATES

H. G. Nicholas

1963
CHATTO & WINDUS
LONDON

Published by
Chatto & Windus Ltd
42 William IV Street
London W.C.2
*
Clarke, Irwin & Co Ltd
Toronto

Printed in Great Britain by
Cox & Wyman Ltd
London Fakenham and Reading

IN MEMORIAM
R. J. C.

CONTENTS

PREFACE

I T is a measure of the intimacy that exists between Britain and the U.S.A. that it does not come naturally to write of British *foreign* policy in a context where the United States is involved. Yet that is what this book is about. It is not a study of Anglo-American relations, nor yet of British public opinion in relation to the U.S.A.; it is an attempt to describe and analyse the dealings of the British Government with the American Government as they have been affected by the changes wrought by the war and the post-war years. It is not a history, but it is written with a conviction that every *post hoc* is in some degree a *propter hoc*; consequently some admixture of historical narrative has been judged indispensable for the analysis. It is highly selective; to write comprehensively of its avowed subject is little less than to write a study of British foreign policy in all its aspects, so many and continuous are the points of contact between the two Governments. Rather than attempt the impossible, I have concentrated on certain topics and areas that seem representative and important, but I am very conscious that it is often a hairbreadth that divides the succinct from the cursory.

Too many kindnesses lie behind the preparation and execution of this book for me to thank all my teachers and benefactors, conscious and unconscious, British and American, here. But I must make mention of my debt to the Leverhulme Foundation and St. Antony's College, Oxford, who inspired it, to the Rockefeller Foundation who encouraged it, and to the John Hopkins University who gave it a most hospitable welcome in its earlier dress as the *Albert Shaw Lectures in Diplomatic History for 1961.*

I

THE POWER RELATIONSHIP

POLICY involves power. The fact that the Anglo-American relationship involves a great deal besides does not alter this primary consideration. Much that has changed in British policy towards the United States between 1938 and 1960 is a reflection of the changing power ratio of the two countries during that period.

A country's strength can be expressed in many ways, and the various components of national power rise or fall in significance according to the purpose and direction in which they are applied. Thus in a context where war is a possibility all other elements of national strength—natural resources, economic potential, etc.—are ultimately reducible to one, the capacity to wage war, and are very properly eliminated from calculation, save where they can be effectively mobilized for military purposes. However, in the relations of states which have completely foresworn war between each other a somewhat different assessment needs to be made of the elements in the power complex. (Not *wholly* different, because such states in relation to the rest of the world will still operate in a Hobbesian environment and this fact will determine much even of their mutual exchanges.) Where "brute" force is ruled out, other kinds of power and influence swell proportionately. Then, almost as in the relationships of social groups and classes within one law-abiding country, assets which are wholly non-convertible into military uses will have an importance and ultimately a power of their own—"mere" riches, high living standards, even the levels of cultural accomplishment. These are tricky elements to incorporate in any calculus and the temptation to eliminate or demote them is correspondingly greater. But since war is as little conceivable between the United Kingdom and the United States as between any states in the world, any realistic assessment of their comparative strengths will have to take some account even of these strictly civilian elements.

With this reminder, let us begin our comparison with the conventional items. The disparity between the British islands and the American sub-continent in area and natural resources is so great and

11

so familiar as not to require any statistical demonstration; indeed, having remained virtually unchanged throughout the period under review, it may more properly be regarded as in the province of geography than of history. The human element in the equation has, however, undergone no small modification since 1938; though in each country the population trend has been continuously upwards the rates of growth in each have been strikingly discrepant:

POPULATION

	U.K.	U.S.A.
1938	47,494,000	129,824,939
1960	52,383,000	179,323,000

From these totals, the two countries at various times put the following numbers into the uniform of their armed services:

SERVICE MANPOWER

	U.K.	U.S.A.
1938	428 thousand	323 thousand
(the last pre-war year)		
1945	4,682 thousand	12,123·5 thousand
(the peak year of World War II)		
1960	526 thousand	2,502 thousand

SERVICE BY SERVICE

ARMY

	U.K.	U.S.A.
1938	226 thousand	185·5 thousand[1]
1945	2,931 „	8,268 „ [1]
1960	264·3 „	881 „

NAVY

	U.K.	U.S.A.
1938	119 thousand	119 + 18 thousand Marines
1945	789 „	3,380 + 475 „ „
1960	97·8 „	628 + 177 „ „

[1] Until 1947 the U.S. Air Force was part of the Army.

AIR FORCE

	U.K.	U.S.A.
		[1]
1938	83 thousand	
1945	963 „	2,282 thousand[1]
1960	163·5 „	816 „

For Britain, as a sea-faring island, another set of figures has an especial relevance here :

MERCHANT MARINE

	U.K.	U.S.A.
1938	160,000 seamen	51,000 seamen
	17,780,000 gross tonnage	12,050,000 gross tonnage
1945	144,000 seamen	158,700 seamen
	17,702,000 gross tonnage	38,500,000 gross tonnage
1960	163,000 seamen	49,153 seamen
	21,131,000 gross tonnage	24,837,000 gross tonnage

It is not easy to provide figures for realistic comparisons of fighting material and equipment owing to rapid technical changes in national armaments, but a few items may be of some significance :

AIRCRAFT

		U.K.	U.S.A.
1938	First-line aircraft	2,000 approx.	1,500 approx.
1960	Strategic bombers	180 approx.	1,700 approx.

DESTROYERS

	U.K.	U.S.A.
1938	149	206
1960	124	702

[1] Until 1947 the U.S. Air Force was part of the Army.

SUBMARINES

	U.K.	U.S.A.
1938	54	90
1960	48 (of which one, the	174 (of which 17 are
	Dreadnought, is	nuclear-powered
	nuclear-powered)	and 3 can fire
		Polaris nuclear
		missiles)

The budget figures of armed service expenditures undoubtedly need to be read in the light of the higher American production costs and the higher rates of American pay, for serviceman and civilian alike. But even with generous allowance made for these discrepancies, the figures are not out of line with the previous tables:

ARMED SERVICE BUDGETS[1]

	U.K.	U.S.A.
1938	£391 million	£231 million
1945	£4,184 million	£22,496 million
1960	£1,616 million	£16,295 million

Defence Budgets as Percentage of Gross National Product

	U.K.	U.S.A.
1938	15%	1%
1945	50%	43%
1960	7·2%	9%

The broad picture revealed by all the foregoing military statistics is clear. For 1938 it is of a Britain whose armed strength, all round, is at least equivalent to that of the United States, and in its immediate applicability to most likely trouble-spots is almost certainly greater. At the peak of their respective war efforts in 1945 American military power far outshone the British in all branches though not by so much as population differences might suggest.

[1] For purposes of comparison, in these and all the tables which follow I have converted dollars into pounds at the rates of $5.00 to £1 in 1938, to $4·00 to £1 in 1945 and $2·80 to £1 in 1960.

14

But whereas for Britain this represented a total mobilization of all resources, human and natural, such as could not possibly be sustained, unaided, for very long, the United States, even at the peak of her war effort, still had unused resources and imperfectly mobilized reserves; she was a giant who had not found it necessary to exert all her strength. By 1960, a "normal" cold war year in which each country was seeking to preserve a balance between its peaceful commitments at home, its peaceful commitments abroad and its expenditure on its own and its allies' defence all over the world, there was a formidable discrepancy in the military might which each of the two powers mustered. In every branch, by every criterion, the gap between the United Kingdom and the United States had widened vastly since 1938. And in fact the figures understate the case. They take no account of the deadliest weapons of all, the nuclear, and of the means of delivering them. For these no reliable figures are available. But of course it is in this respect more than any other that American power exceeds British. And when one adds to offensive potentiality the defensive advantages which space alone can confer, it is apparent that the United States, in this sphere alone, disposes of a strength not only vastly greater in degree but virtually different in kind from that which Britain can command.

If one looks to the economy behind the armaments an interesting contrast emerges. Traditionally (i.e. in the pre-atomic age) the most reliable indices of the armaments potential of any economy were to be found in its steel production and energy consumption. The following tables give the main figures for these :

CRUDE STEEL PRODUCTION

	U.K.	U.S.A.
1938	10,561,000 tons	28,805,000 tons
1960	24,695,000 tons	90,067,000 tons

COAL PRODUCTION

	U.K.	U.S.A.
1938	226,993,000 tons	352,360,500 tons
1960	193,604,000 tons	384,892,900 tons

PETROLEUM CONSUMPTION[1] (thousand metric tons)

	U.K.	U.S.A.
1938	8,831	128,560 (approx.)
1960	39,983	416,000 („)

ELECTRICITY GENERATED (millions of kilowatt hours)

	U.K.	U.S.A.
1938	24,372	116,681
1860	118,848	845,005

For the United Kingdom virtually the whole of the figures for petroleum and a sizeable proportion of the figures for electricity must be read against the reminder that oil is an imported product, requiring foreign exchange in peace and exposed to every hazard in war. Britain's increased reliance on it is therefore an index of diminished independence as well as of increased industrial (and indeed agricultural) efficiency. The U.S.A. by contrast, though preferring to import much of its oil from cheaper sources of supply, could in fact live off its domestic reserves for an indefinite period of time.

In this connexion the high and increasing oil component in the United Kingdom's total fuel consumption must be borne in mind when considering this final set of consumption statistics:

ENERGY CONSUMPTION
(in millions of metric tons of coal equivalent)

	U.K.	U.S.A.
1937	202·45	759·3
1960	240·15	1,387·02

Taking these statistics as a whole, the most striking aspect of them is the way in which the known and obvious discrepancies between British and American strength, as of 1938, in all these traditional components of a war potential have not in fact *so* greatly widened by 1960. The ratios of each item are roughly as follows:

	STEEL	COAL	PETROLEUM	ELECTRICITY	TOTAL ENERGY
1938	1 : 2.75	1 : 1.5	1 : 15	1 : 4.8	1 : 3.75
1960	1 : 3.5	1 : 2	1 : 14	1 : 6.5	1 : 5.75

[1] U.K. figures are available only in terms of weight, U.S. figures only in terms of volume. Only a rough conversion is therefore possible.

Making allowance for the much greater increase in the population of the United States, it would be tempting to conclude that at least in terms of war potential the British economy had kept pace with its transatlantic rival.

But if this were so, what would one make of the following figures?

GROSS NATIONAL PRODUCT

	U.K.	U.S.A.
1938	£5,772 million	£17,045 million
1960	£22,316 „	£179,727 „

For which the ratios are roughly

1938	1 : 4	1960	1 : 8

Even when all possible allowance is made for the pre-war over-valuation of the pound and a possible overvaluation of the dollar, the contrast remains too great to be explained away. Nor can we say that the greater American product is made up of frills and furbelows, while the smaller British one consists of more of the hard stuff with which wars are waged. The observable tastes of the Welfare State and the comparative expenditures of the two countries on armaments will not support such a thesis. The truth, in terms of comparative British and American power, is far otherwise. It is that the revolution since 1945 in the organization of mass destruction has made the old criteria almost wholly obsolete. Weight of steel now counts for less than the precision of transistors; consumption of energy (at least in traditional forms) may be in inverse proportion to total productivity. This makes more difficult than ever the distinction in an economy between sword-making and ploughshare manufacture; the electronics industry provides indiscriminately the raw materials for conspicuous waste, civilian or military style. The so-called "higher" American standard of living does truly reflect not only a greater production of consumer goods of an acceptable kind but also an economy with a greater military potential. It is harder to measure the new ingredients in this potential than the old, if only because the tempo of technical innovation is so prodigious. All the same, and although in a consumers' society such as the United States much is spent which by any and every standard is waste, there is no reason to doubt that the figures for the Gross National Product are a broadly reliable index to comparative British and American war potentials. As such, they reinforce the evidence of the purely military statistics, of a widening gap in the positions, as world powers, of the United Kingdom and the United States.

To this one should add, on the criterion mentioned at the beginning of this chapter, a word of comparison in respect of the purely pacific, non-convertible elements in the economy. The most obvious of these is food and as a rough indication of this one may reasonably take the figures of wheat and meat production:

WHEAT PRODUCTION (thousand metric tons)

U.K.	U.S.A.
1934–8 (average p.a.) 1,743	25,036
1960 3,040	36,750

MEAT PRODUCTION (thousand metric tons)

U.K.	U.S.A.
1936–9 (average p.a.) 1,277	1935–9 (average p.a.) 7,340
1960 1,717	12,805

In a world in which the problem of hunger and the capacity to aid the great populations of backward states loom so large the contrasts here expressed are of considerable significance. British dependence on imported food-stuffs and America's agricultural surplus (capable, of course, of enormous expansion) have an even greater importance for their relative roles in world politics in 1960 than they had in 1938.

To the discrepancies so far observed two qualifications need to be appended. The first is that Britain has always enjoyed certain advantages by comparison with the United States by reason of the efficiencies of operation open to her small, highly integrated, comparatively well-disciplined and smooth-running society. She may be less powerful, but what power she has she can more easily mobilize and focus. This was markedly apparent during the last war when it was possible in Britain to operate and win almost universal acceptance for a comprehensive plan for maximizing the national effort; the U.S.A.'s size, heterogeneity and comparative inexperience involved her in much greater waste and duplication of effort. This contrast has also been apparent to a lesser extent in some aspects of post-war national life, e.g. the comparatively lower running costs and higher efficiency of Whitehall. Yet too much must not be made of an advantage marginal in any case and likely to prove of diminishing value with every year that passes. Not only does the integration of American life proceed apace, but against the diminishing economies of intimacy have to be set the ever-mounting economies of scale, while the certain gains of experience are likely to be more and more offset, in a revolutionary world, by the benefits that probably accrue to innovation and experiment.

The second qualification to be applied to the statistical comparisons is of quite another order. The figures as they stand completely fail to reflect a crucial fact about the United Kingdom past or present, namely that she is not merely an island group moored off the north-east coast of Europe but is also the centre of a world-wide Empire and Commonwealth. Consequently what she could mobilize in terms of men, money, natural resources and industrial and agricultural potential would always be a good deal more than would appear from these merely insular statistics. Perhaps to an American observer in particular this consideration requires to be mentioned, since the elements of unity in the Commonwealth relationship are concealed by the total absence of any Commonwealth constitution and by the wide geographical scattering of all its component members. Furthermore there is no country with whom the members of the Commonwealth are more concerned to establish an independent, bilateral relationship than with the U.S.A. Yet even in the sphere of Anglo-American relations strictly defined they are a factor to be included. Lord Franks has given a hint of the way in which they impinged on his work as U.K. ambassador in Washington in the years 1948 to 1953:

"Every fortnight except in the summer the eight ambassadors of the Commonwealth met in our Embassy to exchange views and consult informally together. We discussed everything, the movement of affairs in the world, the latest phase of American policy —and the opinions of our different countries about them. We did not mince words."[1]

[1] O. Franks, *Britain and the Tide of World Affairs* (London, New York, 1955), p. 17.

19

What flows from such a relationship is clearly incapable of expression in statistical terms. Certainly there is an obvious sense in which the Commonwealth relationship enhances Britain's own power. With the Commonwealth go institutions like the Sterling Area and preferential arrangements which might make the difference between life and death for a trading nation, or facilities, like the Woomera rocket-range or Christmas Island, indispensable to a competitor in the post-war nuclear weapons race. But it is easier to recognize the existence of such factors than to bring them into any power equation. The relevant statistics of each country's power index cannot simply be added to the United Kingdom total, as the steel production of Illinois might be added to that of Pennsylvania; whether or not the United Kingdom can enhance its own strength in any situation which involves the U.S.A. depends upon a range of unpredictables which varies from issue to issue and Commonwealth member to Commonwealth member. Consequently to put these factors into the accounting is hardly practicable; moreover, if they are to be inserted, they must in fairness be accompanied by some items which would go on the opposite side of the ledger. If the Commonwealth brings strength, it also creates responsibilities. There are outposts to be defended, backward territories clamouring for capital, a huge communications network to be maintained. There has to be a Colonial Development Corporation. There is a Colombo Plan. Here again one is moving into the realm of incommensurables. One can only say that the net result is the creation of something considerably different from, and larger than, the mere insular unit which is the British Isles. How different and how much larger will depend upon time and circumstance and will vary too, not only in itself but, what may be almost as important in this context, according to the estimate Americans have of it. In 1938 the American image of it was largely an imperial image already in many respects out of date and tinged with more than a shade of suspicion and hostility; by 1960 the suspicion and hostility had waned, to be replaced generally by an appreciation of the Commonwealth's stabilizing influence in a shaky world, but with the appreciation went more scepticism about the Commonwealth's continuing unity and less disposition to see the Commonwealth as necessarily an addition to Britain's wealth and power.

For all these reasons the Commonwealth must remain an *x*-factor in these statistical comparisons. What it adds is important and even while we fail to measure it we should take care to remember that it is there. But not only is its contribution uncertain in amount; it is also variable in incidence. The Commonwealth is not a set of dependencies to be commanded; it is a set of associations which may or may not be invoked. Its members have their own relations with the United States; they are at once in and out of the direct Anglo-American relationship. For these reasons, though the Commonwealth may affect, it is not going to upset, the balance of power otherwise existing between London and Washington.

Thus when due account is taken of the two qualifications mentioned, the main conclusions remain. They are that Britain is overshadowed, in respect of all the major power components of a modern state, by the United States, and that despite the increase in British economic strength since 1938 the gap between British military and economic capacities and those of the United States has widened continuously from then until now. Why this is not a matter for alarm or despondency, but how nonetheless it has its own importance for the relations of the two countries, is in part the subject-matter of the pages that follow.

2

THE AXIOMS OF BRITISH POLICY

IT is not practicable to say exactly when it became an axiom of British policy that war against the United States was out of the question. It may have been, as some contend, a concomitant of the abandonment of "splendid isolation" at the turn of the century; it may go back to the decision to arbitrate the Alabama Claims and to abide by the results of the arbitration. No doubt it took possession of the public and the bureaucratic minds by degrees and almost, as it were, insensibly. It never took form as a promulgated "Doctrine"; the most lasting amities are not promulgated, they are lived, and their birth is as little a matter of record as their growth. But whenever we may choose to regard this renunciation of war as having become universally accepted in Britain, one characteristic of the British-American relation has been that at all times, even when the two Governments were official enemies, each country's course has had champions in the other. The lines of disagreement have always run within as much as between us. Or, to put it another way, for some elements in each country at all times war with the other has been anathema; the history of Anglo-American relations down to World War I could almost be written in terms of the steady spread of the idea that no disagreement justified a war between Britain and the United States.

This, of course, is a reflection of the obvious fact that since both countries are democracies their relations are ultimately determined by their citizens and that in thinking about each other's country Britons and Americans extend the idea of national interest to cover a host of intangible elements of sentiment and affection. So much do we do this that in Britain (and, I suspect, in the U.S.A. too) it does not come naturally to us to use the term "foreign policy" in an Anglo-American context. "Foreign policy" is something which Britain has in relation to non-English-speaking countries, in Europe, Asia, Latin America, etc. What we have in relation to the United States is something somehow different. It is more nearly analogous to our relationship with the independent members of the Commonwealth, particularly those of European stock. It is com-

↳ Yes. Britain 22 is now a U.S colony in foreign policy, economy + in culture N.B T.V.

posed, for various people in varying degrees, of the identity of race, the shared inheritance, the common speech and, since 1918 and again since 1945, the alliance in arms. The elements are familiar and do not require recapitulation, but it is important to remember that even in the sharpest clash of "national interests", as conventional diplomacy understands the term, these multiple ties and habitudes constitute a unique framework within which the diplomat has to resolve the differences that reach him without resort to force. This is the first, and iron, law of British policy towards the U.S.A.

The negative principle that war with the U.S.A. is unthinkable has, of course, a positive corollary. Since 1775, however, this has not lent itself to as crisp a formulation. The advocates of amity with the U.S.A. have varied in number and enthusiasm and, above all, in the type and degree of intimacy which they have urged. Since the divorce so painfully made absolute at Yorktown, time and circumstance have between them virtually obliterated both the causes of the quarrel and the hard feelings it occasioned. But opinion in Britain has never been agreed as to whether the ideal relationship now to be aimed at is a re-marriage or a let-bygones-be-bygones friendship. It only knows that a special relationship exists. The level of the U.S.A.'s popularity in Britain has risen and sunk, but public attitudes towards the U.S.A., whether approbatory or hostile, have always been tinged with a set of expectations different from those the public entertains in respect of any "foreign" country. Whether the U.S.A. is thought to be acting well or ill, she is judged by a set of standards, moral, Anglo-Saxon, and familial which have more in common with those that would be applied to Canada, Australia, or New Zealand than anything else. This has not necessarily provided British Governments with helpful directives in the framing of official policy where the U.S.A. is involved, since it is notoriously difficult to translate family attitudes into formal statements. But at least since World War I British governments have given the highest priority to establishing and maintaining close understanding with the U.S.A. and this has been accepted by the public as, *ceteris paribus*, a self-justifying explanation of any act of policy. *"Ceteris paribus"* has worn different meanings according to the critic's assessment of Britain's needs and strength, and her precise degree of dependence on the U.S.A. for the attainment of her vital national objectives, but in this century no responsible element in British opinion has ever denied the high value of close amity with the U.S.A.

But while the level of co-operation fluctuated certain principles about its style won common acceptance. The first was the desirability, wherever possible, of avoiding formal, written agreements. This was partly an expression of the easy intimacy that existed; written alliances are made with strangers, friends have no need of codified pledges. It was also a by-product of a tough folk memory, particularly strong on the American side, which regarded all diplomatic agreements as the entangling wiles not merely of a foreign power but of a positively illiberal *ancien régime*, wherever located. The corollary of this was a tradition of frank speaking and an easy exchange of confidences at most levels of government, the political and the bureaucratic. Much depended, of course, on the personalities involved, the topics arising and the mood of the moment, but there existed between London and Washington even in the heyday of American inter-war isolationism a freer traffic of information and consultation than regularly obtained with any other extra-Commonwealth capital. This was accompanied, as was proper to two free countries, by a continuous flow of unofficial comment and consultation in public and in private on each other's affairs so that in some sense there always existed an Anglo-American community of discourse which powerfully affected the behaviour of each Government to the other and to the world outside.

There was a recognition, burnt into the British mind by the Sackville-West incident if by nothing else, that the frank exchange of opinion should stop short of any suggestion of interference in each other's internal party conflicts. Yet it was a paradox of the relationship that its working efficiency was indubitably affected by changes of administration in each country, although the fiction had to be preserved that this was none of either country's business. To a considerable extent, of course, the common interest in co-operation persisted through changing presidencies and premierships but it was undeniable that it made a great deal of difference to the relationship whether there were like-minded régimes in London and Washington or not.

In 1938 like-mindedness was conspicuously absent. Though the reforming impulse of the New Deal had to a large extent spent itself in Washington this was in part at least because its place had been taken by a lively concern for the future of democracy outside the U.S.A. Although there were hesitancies and ambiguities about Roosevelt's foreign policy its main disposition was clear enough, to side with the free countries against the rising menace of the Axis powers. In Britain, on the other hand, there persisted in office a Conservative administration, nominally national, whose reforming ambitions at home had always been extremely modest and whose resistance to tyranny abroad had been spasmodic and inadequate. Between the confident, progressive temper of a Roosevelt who thought he had a "rendezvous with destiny" which he could shape to his own purposes and the cautious conservative disposition of a Chamberlain there was a gigantic gulf of comprehension. How wide it was was catastrophically revealed in an incident in January, 1938.

This was the celebrated proposal which Roosevelt confidentially adumbrated to Chamberlain to call an international conference in Washington to discuss the underlying causes of world tension and to work out possible bases for a settlement. In view of the hold that isolationists had established over American opinion this presidential initiative was a courageous move such as might have been a prelude to the U.S.A. taking her share in the task of keeping the peace. Almost any British prime minister at any time since Versailles would have welcomed it with open arms. To Chamberlain however it appeared as a "bomb" which would explode amidst his own neat plans for European appeasement; or, as he put it to Roosevelt, there would be "a risk of his proposal cutting across our efforts here".[1] In face of this rebuff Roosevelt's initiative withered on the vine, Chamberlain persisting in his attitude even after Eden had made clear his opposition and Sumner Welles had warned the British ambassador, Sir Ronald Lindsay, that "the silence of the British Government (in regard to the plan) might possibly be construed as an indication of apathy on the part of Great Britain".[2]

From some points of view the gap in the thinking of the two Governments was not great. As the leading American historians of the period put it, "it is plain that the President's project . . . was intended to buttress the attempt of Britain to reach agreement with Germany. Though involving no approval of British appeasement,

[1] K. Feiling, *Neville Chamberlain* (London, New York, 1946), p. 336.

[2] *Foreign Relations of the United States, 1938*, Vol. I, p. 125.

it certainly implied acceptance of it".[1] Thus the obstacle to co-operation lay not in a clash of policies but in a clash of temperaments and philosophies. Had Churchill or Eden been Prime Minister, or had the latter's views as Foreign Secretary prevailed, a positive response would have been sent with consequences which are incalculable.

The incident well illustrates, however, the sort of diastole and systole which characterized Anglo-American relations in the thirties. The legacy of World War I was an ever more powerful America swinging between isolationism and an acceptance of her world commitments, and a weakened Britain which alternated between seeking allies and contracting out of her obligations. Had American policy continued on a Wilsonian course Britain's task would have been easy; standing firm in face of Axis threats, Britain would have made the task of the Wilsonians and their successors a great deal simpler. As it was, British appeasers could always contend, as Chamberlain contended, that "it is always best and safest to count on nothing from the Americans but words";[2] at the same time every surrender by British appeasers strengthened the hand of American isolationists in their illogical but potent contention that the United States must not become involved in European disputes in which all the values they cared for were being surrendered without a struggle. In such a situation British diplomacy could make little or no use of the existing habits of consultation and co-operation with the U.S.A., because it was not prepared to make the initial affirmation of purpose around which sympathetic Americans might rally. No doubt a formidable set of isolationist barriers had by 1938 been erected in the U.S.A.—the Johnson Act, the Neutrality Acts, and the sort of mentality which shuddered at Roosevelt's "Quarantine" speech in 1937—but the known sympathies of the President and his advisers should have served in 1938 as they did in 1940 to give British policy a fixed point to steer by. The failure to evolve an effective Anglo-American response to the dictators had its roots in history, in the disappointment over the League, the disagreement over War Debts, the failures of economic co-operation, the rival alibis for the Manchurian fiasco. But it also reflected the

[1] W. L. Langer and S. E. Gleason, *The Challenge to Isolation* (New York, London, 1952), p. 25.

[2] Feiling, op. cit., p. 325.

low tone of British democracy in the thirties, the basically negative and timorous style of British public policy in all its aspects which found it had less in common with the bracing affirmations of the New Deal than with the decadence of the French Third Republic.

If one asks, therefore, what was the place held by the United States in the British Government's world view in 1938 the answer must be that while in principle the importance of American co-operation was recognized, in practice British policy was being directed as if, as a world power, the U.S.A. did not exist. In Europe the problem was to find a way of getting along with the Axis powers, on the assumption that their demands could be met without war and a general settlement reached without bringing either the U.S.A. or the U.S.S.R. into the picture. (Though of course if the U.S.A. could be induced to support British policy its endorsement was welcome—cf. Chamberlain's attempt in January, 1938, to get the U.S.A. to take identical action in recognizing Italy's conquest of Ethiopia. But when, as in this case, the U.S.A. would not conform, and indeed was sharply critical, the United Kingdom went ahead without her.) Outside Europe there was only one theatre in which British policy needed to take serious account of the United States: that was the Far East. Here indeed, as the Brussels Conference of 1937 showed, there was a broad identity of views, a general British willingness to accept an American initiative and a marked reluctance to go a step beyond the United States. As Eden put it, according to Cordell Hull, "Britain would neither attempt to take the lead . . . nor push the United States out in front, but . . . would base her policy on American policy".[1] Since the U.S.A. was determined not to assume any commitments which would arouse isolationist suspicion, no joint action was taken. The most that the United States would ever agree to was action "concurrently" and "on parallel lines"—phrases that recur again and again in this context. In a crisis even this could not be guaranteed. Thus when in December, 1937, the United States gunboat *Panay* was sunk by Japanese planes near Nanking the United States protest was delivered independently, with no attempt to concert with Britain whose gunboat, the *Ladybird*, had also been damaged in the same attack.

Perhaps the paradoxical character of Anglo-American relations at this time is best expressed in the messages which passed between

[1] Cordell Hull, *Memoirs*, Vol. I (New York, 1948), p. 553.

Chamberlain and Roosevelt in 1937 about a possible visit by the Prime Minister to the United States. The proposal appears to have originated with Roosevelt in July that Chamberlain should visit Washington "as soon as conditions appear to warrant your doing so" to discuss Anglo-American "co-operation in the promotion of economic stability and peace in the world". Chamberlain appears to have accepted in principle, but to have stressed the importance of "proper preparation" and "timing".[1] A follow-up letter came from Roosevelt asking for further suggestions as to useful preparatory steps. Then six weeks seem to have elapsed while Chamberlain, partly on holiday and partly at home, ruminated his rejoinder; when he finally replied on 28 September it was in supremely negative terms: "I am afraid I cannot suggest any way in which the meeting between us could be expedited, though I greatly regret this both on personal and official grounds." Most extraordinary, however, was the reasoning which preceded this conclusion—that while in Europe there was an easing of tension, in the Far East the situation "justified our worst fears" and that he saw "little prospect at the present time of being able to improve it by action on the part of the Western Powers".[2] In other words, whether things were improving, as in Europe, or deteriorating, as in the Far East, the conclusion was the same—that the concerting of policy with the U.S.A. was not a serious objective of British statesmanship.

Thus amity with the United States was not so much ignored as taken for granted. In a world view which involved a kind of British isolationism where mainland Europe was concerned and a cultivation of her extra-European and imperial gardens, American acquiescence in such a policy was tacitly assumed. Thus Mr. Joseph Kennedy (the United States ambassador) reported to Washington a conversation which he held with Lord Halifax on 12 October, 1938: "First of all, Halifax does not believe that Hitler wants to have a war with Great Britain and he does not think there is any sense in Great Britain having a war with Hitler unless there is direct interference with England's Dominions [sic]. The future of England, as he sees it, is to strengthen herself in the air . . . Then after that to let Hitler go ahead and do what he likes in Central Europe . . . Therefore he sees the future of England lies in her maintaining her relations in the Mediterranean, keeping friendly

[1] *Foreign Relations of the United States 1937*, Vol. I, p. 113.
[2] Ibid., pp. 136–7.

with Portugal, he hopes Spain, Greece, Turkey, Egypt, Palestine . . . plus England's connexions in the Red Sea, fostering the Dominion connections, and staying very friendly with the United States, and then, as far as everything else is concerned, Hitler can do the best he can for himself."[1]

Fortunately this attitude did not obtain at all levels in the Government. Not only did Eden, as his resignation in 1938 evinced, hold a different opinion about the imperative necessity of working with the United States, but Whitehall at the official levels kept fairly steadily in mind the importance of consultation and, wherever possible, co-operation with their American opposite numbers. Otherwise the prospect of effective co-operation when the hour and the will were propitious would have been slight indeed.

Rooted as it was in the conviction that appeasement would bring peace, the government's policy of comparative indifference to co-operation with the U.S.A. underwent a marked change after Munich when appeasement was found to be a sham and war began to appear inescapable. If there was to be a war in Europe it was apparent even to Chamberlain that American aid would be needed to win it. Then when, on 4 January, 1939, Roosevelt frankly warned that "there are many methods short of war, but stronger and more effective than mere words, of bringing home to aggressor Governments the aggregate sentiments of our people", Chamberlain told Kennedy that he welcomed the pronouncement as having brought about Hitler's "quieting down".[2] When, so far from having quieted down, Hitler proceeded to seize what was left of Czechoslovakia, and Chamberlain was led to make the sudden announcement of Britain's pledge to Poland, his stimulus for so acting, if we may believe Kennedy, derived equally from popular British protests against appeasement, demand for an effective peace front and fear of American criticisms. At about the same time, 21 March, Halifax suggested to Kennedy that if the United States Atlantic fleet could be moved back to San Diego it would lighten the pressure of Pacific policing upon the British, who were unable to spare vessels from the Mediterranean to go to Singapore. The President complied and the move was not lost on the Japanese.

In June this positive soliciting of American co-operation was

[1] Op. cit., *1938*, Vol. I, pp. 85–86.

[2] Langer and Gleason, op. cit., p. 59.

symbolized in the visit to Washington of the King and Queen (the idea had originally been hatched in 1937). More practically, it found expression in the announcement in April of the appointment as British ambassador of Philip Kerr, Lord Lothian. This brought to the embassy in August what it had not had for some years, a public figure in his own right who had a deep conviction of the primacy of Anglo-American understanding and a capacity for conveying this beyond mere diplomatic circles to the American press and public outside. When, by the summer, war in Europe was, to almost every clear-sighted eye, inescapable, Britain responded quickly to the President's suggestion that in order to enable the U.S.A. in time of war to mount a neutrality patrol 300 miles out to sea the American navy and aircraft should be allowed to use the harbour facilities of Trinidad, Santa Lucia and Bermuda. In all this there was a tacit pro-ally cast to the "neutrality" involved. The object of the patrol was to be the collection of information on belligerent activities, particularly submarine activities, within the patrol zone and no one needed to be told whose submarines would be exposed to detection and which side would benefit from receipt of such information. Unfortunately, of course, there were limits to the extent to which the mantle of neutrality could be stretched in the allies' favour and the Roosevelt administration's attempt to get the Neutrality Act revised to permit the allies to obtain arms on a "cash and carry" basis was frustrated by a group of Congressmen who knew better than the President that there would be no war in Europe that summer. All the same this did not prevent the State and War Departments, as well as the White House, giving every encouragement even before September, 1939, to the proposal for establishing an official British Purchasing Agency in the United States.

The outbreak of war accelerated the drive for American aid and co-operation rather than introducing any new element into British policy towards the U.S.A. Before decisive shifts in the scale or degree of intimacy could occur two things were needed, the substitution for Chamberlain of a British leader who could really command the confidence and respect of the American President and his administration, and a break-through in the long and, as it seemed from London, painfully slow battle against the forces of American isolationism. As it turned out, the two developments occurred virtually simultaneously, precipitated by the success of the German offensive in the spring of 1940. The German triumph in Norway, in bringing Churchill to power gave the shaping of British policy to a man who had always held co-operation with the U.S.A. to be a precondition of victory in war or success in peace. The sudden awareness created by Dunkirk of what a British defeat might mean for the U.S.A. enabled Roosevelt to effect the destroyer-bases deal, and initiate lend-lease and the policy of "all aid short of war" which were the foundations of the Anglo-American wartime alliance.

3

THE WARTIME ALLIANCE AND AFTER

IN a notable passage in his *Second World War* Churchill describes his reaction to the news of Pearl Harbor:

"So we had won after all! Yes, after Dunkirk; after the fall of France; after the horrible episode of Oran; after the threat of invasion, when, apart from the Air and the Navy, we were an almost unarmed people; after the deadly struggle of the U-boat war—the Battle of the Atlantic, gained by a hand's breath; after seventeen months of lonely fighting and nineteen months of my responsibility in dire stress, we had won the war. England would live; Britain would live; the Commonwealth of Nations and the Empire would live. How long the war would last or in what fashion it would end, no man could tell, nor did I at this moment care. Once again in our long island history we should emerge, however mauled or mutilated, safe and victorious. We should not be wiped out. Our history would not come to an end. We might not even have to die as individuals. Hitler's fate was sealed. Mussolini's fate was sealed. As for the Japanese, they would be ground to powder. All the rest was merely the proper application of overwhelming force . . . Many disasters, immeasurable cost and tribulation lay ahead, but there was no doubt about the end."[1]

The assurance of American aid embodied in Lend-Lease had perhaps been a guarantee that in this worst of her wars Britain would not be defeated, but only America's actual entry into the fight on Britain's side provided the assurance that Britain would actually win. The awareness, after the fall of France, that victory depended on the U.S.A. sank deep into the consciousness of every Briton and lay behind every major decision that the Government took from that time onwards. To secure the closest possible co-

[1] *The Second World War*, Vol. III (London, 1959) pp. 539–40, (New York, 1960) pp. 606–7.

operation of the U.S.A. in our war effort became, next to the defeat of Hitler itself, the main objective of British policy.

The realization of this objective was enormously facilitated by the profound mutual respect and strong personal attachment that marked the relations of the two national leaders, Churchill and Roosevelt, but it did not have to rely upon the personalities at the top. A profound identity of thinking about the nature of the struggle and about the ultimate issues involved underlay the policies of both Governments at most levels and was itself a reflection of common elements in the habits and beliefs of the two nations. This made possible a wartime alliance which was a real merging of two national wills, two fighting forces and two economies. The partnership in arms worked not through an agreed division of labour so much as through a sharing of burdens and a genuine merging of national identities of which S.H.A.E.F. (Supreme Headquarters Allied Expeditionary Force) was the supreme exemplification. The joint military effort was underpinned by a wholly unprecedented pooling of national resources. This is the phenomenon to which Churchill referred when he spoke of "our affairs . . . becoming rather mixed up". It was exemplified in the development of Lend-Lease into Mutual Aid, it was enshrined in the institution of the Combined Boards, and given perhaps its most explicit expression in the terms of reference of the Combined Production and Resources Board: "The Board shall combine the production programmes of the United States and the United Kingdom into a single integrated programme, adjusted to the strategic requirements of the war."[1] And of course this pooling concept extended into the realm of techniques and ideas, of which radar, atomic energy, military and political intelligence are only the most obvious examples.

The pooling involved in the joint war effort was always a little more real for Britain than for the U.S.A. There were always American leaders who would tolerate no British interference in their theatres, like Admiral King in the Pacific; British generalissimi might be difficult, like Montgomery, but they could never ignore their yoke-fellows. The American economy, rich and sprawling, never came under the same degree of effective Government direction and control that the British knew from 1940 onwards; consequently there was never an equivalent degree of conversion from

[1] *Documents on American Foreign Relations, 1941–2*, p. 250.

peacetime to wartime requirements. More than this, the U.S.A., who in many fields of services and production supplied Britain's needs as well as her own, had a freedom which Britain lacked to decide which of the elements of her contribution should go into the common pool.

Nevertheless not only did the system genuinely work, to a surprising degree; it was also in Britain's obvious interest, as the weaker and poorer partner, both to preserve the system and, even where it cracked, to maintain belief in it. In Britain it sank deep roots into the national consciousness where it intertwined itself inextricably with the concept of "fair shares" on which increasingly the morale of the British home front came to depend. It made smooth a partnership with a rich and remote ally which had, in the abstract, all the elements that make for fratricidal strife. Personified in Eisenhower, it was immensely popular at all levels, civilian and military. The alliance, so conceived, interpenetrated the national life at every point; it was civil servants learning that "restricted" was the American for "confidential"; it was Grosvenor Square turning into Eisenhower Platz; it was G.I.s in the village pub; it was SPAM. Like the war itself, it was all-pervasive. Its detailed history does not require telling here; it was indeed in large part the history in its later stages of the war itself.

In proportion as the war was total, so the transition to peace, as far as Britain was concerned, was gradual. Too gradual perhaps, but circumstances and a strong demand for social justice combined to make it so. A nation whose life, in all its aspects, had been dedicated to waging war could no more revert at once to peacetime normality than a man whose legs have been tied can walk the moment his cords have been cut. And just as the war persisted in British thinking, so did expectations and habits bred of the alliance.

To preserve the essence of the alliance in the post-war world had become a major British war aim. As the hoped-for intimacy with the U.S.S.R. failed to materialize, as indeed it became obvious that Stalin wanted a European settlement radically different from that which British obligations and interests dictated, so the desire to retain American strength and support in Europe came to dominate British thinking. By 1945 it was abundantly true, as the leading historian of the alliance put it, that "Churchill's greatest fear was that the United States would abandon Europe after the war, leaving Great Britain to face Soviet Russia alone with nothing more than

34

her own resources and whatever Continental allies could be created".[1] To avert such a catastrophe Britain cheerfully waived several of her preferences in the planning of a world organization and accepted at all important points the American design, as well as an American site for the United Nations once it had been created. But the fear of a revived American isolationism did not end with the assurance of United States membership in the United Nations. The premature death of Roosevelt, his legacy of trust in Stalin's good intentions, the alarming indifference of the American military to the political implications of their actions in Central Europe, for example over the determination of the east-west boundary lines in Germany and Austria—all this kept British anxieties alive. To retain the U.S.A. as a close partner with Britain seemed the only way to avert the perils which post-war Europe seemed to present.

In the U.S.A., unfortunately, very different thinking prevailed about the transition from war to peace and its implications for the alliance. The overwhelming majority of Americans, whether isolationists or not, were agreed on making a clear-cut distinction between war and peace. War was killing, or being killed by, Germans and Japanese. When the fighting was over the war ceased, the troops came back home and the other abnormalities associated with war came to an end too. Mr. Truman was only speaking the truth about his fellow-countrymen when he claimed that "no people in history have been known to disengage themselves so quickly from the ways of war".[2] This divergence of attitudes and expectations had immediate implications for the alliance. A week after V-J Day Mr. Truman announced the ending of Lend-Lease; by the end of the war, as a logical corollary of the bonfire of American domestic controls, the whole structure of Anglo-American economic "pooling" was in ruins; the Combined Food Board alone was left going until December, 1946. The military disintegration was a little less explicit, but no less real. The Combined Chiefs of Staff were not indeed formally wound up; they ceased nonetheless to exist, except for dealing with Trieste and a few other residual side-issues.

For a moment it seemed to the British as if all the firm realities of the bilateral alliance were being washed away in a flood of wishful multilateralism. For the intimate political consultations of

[1] W. H. McNeill, *America, Britain and Russia, 1941–1946* (London, New York, 1953), p. 411.

[2] H. S. Truman, *Memoirs*, I (New York, London, 1955), p. 506.

F.D.R. and the "Former Naval Person" would be substituted the publicized deadlocks of the Foreign Ministers' Conference; the solid shield of the Anglo-American forces would be replaced by the never-to-be-actualized police functions of the United Nations Security Council; instead of the orderly apparatus of economic pooling and planning there would be a free for all tempered only by the aspirations of an international trade convention and the charity of U.N.R.R.A. To make matters worse, not only did the Americans appear to think that these would be effective substitutes for the alliance; many of them, inside the administration as well as without, had come to regard the alliance as a positive obstacle to the *novus ordo saeclarum.* To think in terms of an Anglo-American alliance was, in the view of a good many, to think in anti-Soviet terms, to be impairing the harmony of American-Soviet relations, on which the real hopes of future peace depended, in order to preserve a fighting partnership whose justification was now ended. Was there not even some support for this view to be constructed out of the fragmentary political testament of the late Franklin Roosevelt himself? Thus when the institutions of the new order failed to function as hoped there was even a certain disposition to try and remedy this by an ostentatious disavowal of the old alliance. The battles in the infant United Nations in early 1946 over Iran, Indonesia, Greece, Lebanon and Syria were mainly fought out by Bevin and Molotov with Byrnes often playing the role of mediator and pacifier. Even after President Truman himself had become tired, as he put it, of "babying the Soviets" it was left to his English visitor, Winston Churchill, in his Fulton speech to sound the call for the west to unite and face the full measure of the Soviet threat. Moreover, though the speech received private encouragement and applause from the highest circles in the United States, public official endorsement was still thought inadvisable.

Some of the British alarm of 1945 turned out to be exaggerated. The ending of Lend-Lease turned out in fact to be somewhat less abrupt than Mr. Truman's staccato announcement made it appear. The pipe-line provided time in which to negotiate the economic aid from North America which was embodied in the Anglo-American and the Anglo-Canadian Loan Agreements of December, 1945. Securing this aid was an imperative for Britain hardly less pressing than the maintenance of American co-operation in the political and diplomatic spheres. The war left Britain impoverished and at many

36

points crippled. The sheer physical destruction she had sustained was considerable—£1,500 million on shore in property losses and £700 million at sea in the sinking of one-third of her merchant fleet. Of her overseas investments £1,118 million had been liquidated, while her gold and dollar reserves had dropped from £864 million in 1938 to £453 million in 1945. Meanwhile her external liabilities in the form of debts mainly in the sterling area had risen from £760 million to £3,355 million. In all one could estimate that about one-quarter (£7,300 million) of Britain's pre-war national wealth had been lost in the war. At the same time her export trade was down to thirty per cent of its 1938 volume in a world in which the cost of imports had risen by fifty per cent. Only America could physically provide the goods and raw materials necessary to keep life going and rebuild the battered industries; only America could provide the economic wherewithal.

Yet here again the tenacious grip of wartime experience and wartime ways of thinking put the British at odds with an America which wanted to treat the war as a closed book, indeed a closed ledger. This was not just the view of the man in the street; it was if anything even more the blinkers in which nearly six years of war had fastened the best minds in Whitehall. It was that restless innovator and fertile genius Lord Keynes who wished above all to rest the British proposals for economic aid on the argument of what Britain had suffered in the common cause and what the principle of equality of sacrifice would dictate in a final reckoning. "Since," as he said, "our transitory financial difficulties are largely due to the role we played in the war, and to the costs we incurred before the United States entered the war, we here in London feel . . . that it might not be asking too much of our American friends that they should agree to see us through the transition by financial aid which approximated to a grant."[1] In relation to the wartime concept of "pooling" such an approach could be justified. One major reason for Britain's plight in 1945, was that, though a trading nation, she had, as part of the mutually agreed production plan, switched her export industries to munitions work and also scrupulously abstained from using any Lend-Lease materials for manufacturing export goods. It could be shown, insofar indeed as figures can ever demonstrate such propositions, that, man for man, the British had suffered more in the common struggle than the Americans; it could be

[1] H. L. Deb. Vol. 138, col. 779–780, 10 December, 1945.

37

argued that much was due in respect of the period before Pearl Harbor when Britain "stood alone".

In line with this kind of reasoning the Treasury prepared a White Paper setting out what Britain had done and suffered in the common cause and for three days in the Washington negotiations Keynes expounded the case for an outright grant based upon it. But what seemed obvious and fair in London wore a different appearance in Washington. As Keynes himself put it on his return, justifying the financial agreements before a sceptical House of Lords: "But what a gulf separates us from the climate of Washington; and what a depth of misunderstanding there will be as to what governs relations between even the friendliest and most like-minded nations if we imagine that so free and easy an arrangement could commend itself to the complex politics of Congress or to the immeasurably remote public opinion of the United States. Nevertheless, it was on these lines that we opened our case. For three days the heads of the American delegation heard me expound the material. . . . Nevertheless, it was not very long before the British delegation discovered that a primary emphasis on past services and past sacrifices would not be fruitful. The American Congress and the American people have never accepted any literal principle of equal sacrifice, financial or otherwise, between all the allied participants. . . . We soon discovered, therefore, that it was not our past performance or our present weakness but our future prospects of recovery and our intention to face the world boldly that we had to demonstrate. Our American friends were interested not in our wounds, though incurred in the common cause, but in our convalescence."[1]

The reassuring implications of the final twist of Keynes's closing epigram were not fully borne out by the financial settlements which were eventually concluded. Even Keynes could not disguise his disappointment at the final form of the Agreements and it was less his advocacy than inexorable necessity—Britain simply had to have the dollars—that induced Parliament to ratify them after a division in which 169 M.P.s abstained from voting, Churchill amongst them. It was not merely that the Agreements were felt to be ungenerous (this, after all, was an issue on which the British judgment might reasonably be thought to be suspect); what most worried their critics was their multilateralism. Here, in the convertibility

[1] Op. cit. col. 780–782.

clauses, in the links between the loan and the acceptance of the Bretton Woods institutions, in the whole concept of Britain's problem being just that of negotiating a quick transition to full multilateralism—in all this there was a very explicit substitution of the new, untried world of international institutions for the familiar and trusted wartime alliance. The economists had gone even farther than the diplomats and the politicians in moving Anglo-American relations from their old moorings. There were many who argued, Keynes amongst them, that in this open sea lay Britain's truest safety, that Britain's destiny as a trading nation was ultimately bound up with the maintenance of an international system of trade and convertibility. They were the counterparts of the positive champions of the United Nations who saw the organization as the natural expression of the interest in peace and international order which Britain and the United States had in common. But just as the dry powder school wished to maintain within the United Nations framework the working mechanism of the diplomatic and military Atlantic alliance, so even amongst the economic liberals there was a gloomy conviction that the new international economic institutions could not sustain the weight that the Anglo-American Financial Agreements imposed on them. They were right; it was not the Bank and the Fund which took over the unfinished business of the American loan, but Marshall Aid. At the same time, by a curious paradox, the Financial Agreements did, as it turned out, provide the most striking demonstration that the realities of the Anglo-American alliance had in fact survived.

The passage of the Agreements through the British Parliament was not, of course, sufficient to bring them into operation. To become effective they had to be approved by the body which alone could authorize the expenditure, the American Congress. And in fact their passage through that body was, for different reasons, no less painful and a great deal more prolonged than it had been in Britain. For months throughout the spring and early summer of 1946 while Britain, the proud mendicant, half hoped, half feared that Congress would reject them, the debate dragged on, generating its inevitable accompaniment of mutual resentment and ill-feeling. The arguments of its supporters in the executive branch about the brave new world of multilateralism and free convertibility were poorly received in a chamber whose composition gives the maximum scope to every advocate of economic nationalism—so poorly indeed that it looked as if its prospects would founder. Fortunately, as the months dragged on, economic nationalism was overborne, not by the new liberalism, but by lively fears of what Russia was doing to the Western world on the diplomatic and political fronts. Eventually it was nothing less than the old alliance argument which carried the day. Recognizing the strength of the opposition and the cruciality of the vote Sam Rayburn, the Speaker of the House, left the chair to make a rare personal intervention. His argument was simple and, as it proved, decisive: "I do not want Western Europe, England, and all the rest pushed toward an ideology that I despise. I fear that if we do not co-operate with this great natural ally of ours that is what will happen . . . If we are not allied with the British democracy I fear someone will be and God pity us when we have no ally across the Atlantic Ocean and God pity them too."[1]

[1] 92 *Congressional Record 9040*, (12 July, 1946.)

4

THE COLD WAR ALLIANCE

IT could be said at the end of 1946 that the Anglo-American alliance was in an ambiguous condition. On the one hand its formal structure had disintegrated with the end of the war; on the other hand a good deal of its spirit persisted, exemplified in a resolute British endeavour to keep the U.S. *engagé* and in an American recognition that Britain constituted, for practical purposes, her most reliable friend. What degree of American commitment could be secured and what mutual obligations the friendship would entail were, however, still uncertain. The resolution of these uncertainties was the work of the years 1947, 1948 and 1949.

It is not necessary to re-tell the whole story of the adoption of the Truman Doctrine, the shaping of the Marshall Plan and the evolution of N.A.T.O. But some features of the story are necessary to a full understanding of the relationship which Britain built up with the U.S. in these years. When in late February, 1947, Britain formally notified the U.S.A. that she could no longer continue to be the reservoir of financial-military support for Greece and Turkey it is doubtful if the full implications of the act were as clearly grasped in Whitehall as in Washington. Superficially it was a matter of $250 million which Britain, in the hard-pressed winter of 1947, could no longer afford. The decision to place the last straw in America's lap seems to have come, like so many fateful British decisions, from the Treasury. The news of the decision initially created relatively little stir in Britain. Indeed it was not until 5 March that news of the British abdication was at all prominently displayed to British readers, and then only in the form of a dispatch from Washington. It was 17 March before a statement was made in the House of Commons. It excited comparatively little comment. What in retrospect may appear a milestone in Anglo-American relations was generally viewed at the time as only a minor adjustment in the load of British post-war commitments. That it would result in a "Truman Doctrine" seems to have been totally unexpected in Britain. Possibly this was because it was only relatively, not absolutely, that it represented a lightening of that load. Only a

41

little more than three months earlier, on 6 November, 1946, Mr. Attlee had announced that the rate of demobilization in the services would be slowed down, so that the number of men under arms at the year's end would be 1,427,000 instead of the 1,200,000 originally planned. And on the same day that Mr. Truman spoke to Congress the British Government published the draft of their bill to perpetuate conscription on the basis of an eighteen-month period of service.

What was happening, of course, was that the Russians were raising the pressure on the British defence line just at a time when *all* economic considerations demanded a cutting of our cloth. Nineteen forty-six had ended with deadlock over Germany and 1947 began with the mockery of "free elections" in Poland. No foreign minister could advise his colleagues that the nation could relax its guard, but in view of the rate at which the American loan was disappearing and the imbalance of payments worsening there had to be a reduction of overseas military expenditure. (Critics pointed out that the £300 million spent on maintaining our overseas responsibilities, mostly in Germany and the Middle East, exactly equalled the gap in the balance of payments.) The solution was not so much to reduce as to shift the burden; to spend, if it must be, more at home, but to unload some of the overseas tasks on to the U.S.A. By one of history's pretty ironies the first burden to be transferred to Uncle Sam's shoulders was the one which, two or three years earlier, John Bull had been most severely censured for assuming—Greece, where Churchill's anti-Communist intervention had won sharp "anti-imperialist" rebukes in the U.S.A. in 1944 and 1945.

One cannot say with confidence how far the Government at this moment was working on the assumption that the alliance *à trois* with the U.S.S.R. was dead and that an outright, explicit Anglo-American front should take its place. As late as 22 December, 1946, Ernest Bevin had depicted Britain as "midway" between the U.S.A. and the U.S.S.R., "not tying herself to anyone" and, when Stalin alleged that this meant Britain was welshing on the Anglo-Soviet Treaty, Bevin agreed to "reaffirm" the Treaty a month later. But though Bevin undoubtedly did not wish to close the door on a European settlement with the U.S.S.R., his public statements have to be read in the light of his anxiety, as a Labour Foreign Secretary, over maintaining unity in a party with a vociferous left wing.

42

There is no reason to doubt that for all practical purposes the British Government had given up hope of any better relationship with the U.S.S.R. than one of peaceful containment and that since the war's end there had never been any faltering in their desire to have the closest possible relationship with the U.S.A. At the same time it would seem that British official circles were surprised and a little taken aback at the challenging tone of Mr. Truman's message; there is reason to suppose that no one expected the burden which was so quietly dropped to be picked up quite so resoundingly.

Despite the drama of 12 March, 1947, what actually happened was very much less than a substitution of *Pax Americana* for *Pax Britannica.* There was no neat and swift switch-over from British to United States responsibility. Far from it. In the first place the United States was by no means in a position to assume such a role. After Mr. Truman's speech there ensued over two months of Congressional debate. Not until 22 May did Mr. Truman sign the Greco-Turkish Aid Bill and when it became law it merely pledged cash for military and economic aid, while providing for missions, military and naval, of an advisory character. There was no provision for the dispatch of troops. When the Greek situation reached a crisis in June and July, 1947, under pressure from the Yugoslavs, Bulgarians and Albanians, the line had to be held without any United States forces. Indeed the first shiploads of United States military material did not arrive until 14 August. Meanwhile Britain was under steady pressure from the United States administration not to withdraw her forces, first of all on the grounds of the anticipated delay in passing the Greco-Turkish Aid Bill, and subsequently in view of the persistently critical situation in Greece. However, the dollar drain accelerated alarmingly in the summer, leading Britain to make renewed announcements of the withdrawal of her forces, announcements which in turn provoked a critical reaction in Washington. Forrestal's diary entry for 4 August indicates how one such communication was received:

"Lunch today with Marshall, Harriman, Snyder. Marshall expressed his deep concern with the implications that might be drawn from the withdrawal of British troops from Greece and Italy. He has wired Bevin in strong language, protesting against the British action in presenting the United States with such decisions as the one of last February advising us that we would have to accept the responsibility for Greece and this most recent one of complete withdrawal from southern Europe. He asked Douglas to inquire of Bevin whether this indicates a fundamental change in British policy. Bevin replied to this in the negative."[1]

In response to pressure such as this, but with great reluctance, Britain left 5,000 men in Greece until well into 1948 and 3,000 or so from then on. The last British troops did not leave Greece until the beginning of 1950.

The fact was that, quite apart from the political difficulty of sending United States troops to Greece, there were hardly the troops available to send. With the expiry of the Selective Service Act on 31 March, 1947, Congress allowed the last relics of military conscription to disappear, not to reappear until in June of the following year, 1948, a fresh Selective Service Act was passed.

Meanwhile, however, the reduction of United Kingdom commitments went on. Although in November, 1946, the Government announced their intention to continue conscription from 1 January, 1949 (when it was due to expire), in April, 1947, they responded swiftly to pressure from their back-benchers and cut the proposed duration from eighteen months to twelve months. On 30 July, 1947, a speed-up in demobilization was ordered and on 30 August, 1947, as part of dollar crisis economies, Attlee announced a further cut which would bring the army down to 1,007,000 by 31 March, 1948. This was further cut in December, 1947, to 937,000 by the same date, while defence estimates published the following February, 1948, envisaged a further reduction of 220,000 within the next year, and a cut of two-ninths in the defence budget, equivalent to £200 million. The retreat from omnicompetence was on.

Undoubtedly the need to trim commitments also had a good deal to do at about the same time with the decision to wind up the costly and thankless Palestine mandate. The United States' repeated refusals (last in November, 1946), to accept any joint responsibility there led to the British Government's decision to hand the problem over to the United Nations. When the United Nations voted for partition in November, 1947, the United States supported it but would not assist in enforcing it. The United Kingdom took the same position, announcing it would withdraw its troops by 1

[1] *The Forrestal Diaries* (London, 1952), pp. 292–3; (New York, 1951), pp. 301–2.

August, 1948. In fact, the first withdrawals occurred on 16 November, 1947; in January, 1948, the Government announced that Britain would terminate its mandate on 15 May, 1948. On 19 March, the United States suddenly announced abandonment of support for partition, in favour of United Nations trusteeship. When the question was raised inside the U.S. administration, how far the United States would or could implement this, it turned out that there simply were not any troops available. Forrestal reports a depressing meeting on 4 April with the Joint Chiefs of Staff which ended on an almost pathetic note: "It was suggested that the British might undertake to hold the fort alone pending the augmentation of our forces, following the adoption of Selective Service."[1] But the United Kingdom was not to be turned aside from its course. The mandate ended, the Jewish Agency proclaimed a Jewish State, eleven minutes later, on 15 May, Mr. Truman accorded it American recognition, and on 30 June, 1948, the last United Kingdom troops left.

From all of which it can be seen that if Anglo-American relations had simply consisted of the United Kingdom passing the sceptre of world responsibility into United States hands the process would have been attended with a good deal of bitterness and re-crimination, and, what is more, the sceptre might well in fact have fallen in the passing. Fortunately this was not what happened. Instead a new basis of United Kingdom–United States collaboration was found in a European, or to be more accurate, North Atlantic and Mediterranean, context.

In retrospect the crucial developments of 1947–8 emerge as logical steps in the evolution of an anti-Russian alliance. And as such indeed they were conceived—all of them by some people, and some of them by all people, but not every one by everybody. Even the Truman Doctrine, though immediately provoked by blatant Communist (even if not overtly Soviet) hostilities against Greece and by Soviet pressure against Turkey, was not approved by the United States Senate until Senator Vandenberg had inserted his proviso that the aid should cease whenever the General Assembly or the Security Council should decide that action taken by the United Nations rendered United States aid unnecessary or undesirable—and that, in a Security Council vote on such an issue, the United States should waive her veto. In both Britain and the U.S.A.

[1] Ibid (London), p. 388; (New York) p. 411.

there was a body of opinion, not necessarily made up of fellow travellers, which felt uneasy at the too openly anti-Russian tone of the Doctrine and wished to stress its essentially defensive implications. That is not to say that anyone in the Government or any but a few far Leftists *disapproved* of the policy; they were merely worried lest it should go too far too roughly. In line with this fear there was a good deal of elaboration of a distinction of which more was to be heard later, between a British policy allegedly aimed at curbing Russian imperialism and an American one which saw the enemy as Communism *per se*.

In this context the Marshall Plan, aired at Harvard on 5 June, three months after the Truman Doctrine had been promulgated on 12 March, was especially attractive to the United Kingdom. In the first place it was an American initiative and invitation. In the second place it was aid that took an economic, not a military form. "Reconstruction" was its theme. And in the third place it was not overtly anti-Russian: "Any Government that is willing to assist in the task of recovery will find full co-operation . . . on the part of the United States Government."[1] The economic emphasis was particularly attractive to Ernest Bevin and though it is very doubtful whether he ever believed the Soviets would join in (except perhaps to wreck it)[2] their inclusion in the invitation undoubtedly helped to solidify Labour support for the plan.

In fact, of course, the Marshall proposals brought not peace but a sword. Invited to confer at Paris, Molotov insisted on individual approaches to the United States and no joint European effort. He warned France and Britain against an action which "could lead to no good". Bevin replied: "My country has faced grave consequences and threats before, and it is not the sort of prospect which will deter us from doing what we consider to be our duty." Thus, ironically, what was a pacific and economic offer come to be a touchstone according to which countries were identified with the American or the Russian camp. Marshall Aid became, under this Russian pressure, a first but quite decisive step towards the unifica-

[1] Mr. Marshall at Harvard. U.S. Dept. of State *Bulletin*, Vol. 16, p. 1159.

[2] Though he did say in a speech in London on 13 June that it would "throw a bridge to link East and West".

tion of Western Europe under British leadership as a pro-American *bloc*.[1]

This role of British leadership in a European approach to the United States was emphasized when the sixteen nations conference met at Paris on 12 July by Bevin being in the chair and later by Sir Oliver Franks becoming chairman of the Committee of European Economic Co-operation (C.E.E.C.) which met and produced an outline European recovery programme by 22 September.[2]

While the future of the Marshall programme was thus back in the lap of the United States, and more specifically of the American Congress, the Russians were making clear to the world the hostile interpretation they put on it. While Communist Parties in Western Europe were trying to overthrow pro-Marshall Governments the Cominform was formed (announcement on 5 October) and the Foreign Ministers' autumn meeting in London, like all its predecessors, stalled under Soviet intransigence. In the middle of December the United States gave interim aid to France, Italy and Austria and by a new agreement with the United Kingdom relieved her of all dollar expenditure in Germany, as well as assuming seventy-five per cent of the cost of both zones.

Thus the division between East and West was becoming more and more explicit. But it was also becoming apparent that if Western Europe was to survive its collective defence would have to be organized. How far British initiative in this was dove-tailed with American thinking at the very earliest stages we do not know. But by 13 January, 1948, Bevin was airing his intentions to the United States in terms which Mr. Truman describes as follows:

"Ernest Bevin, the British Foreign Secretary, had informed Secretary of State Marshall as early as 13 January, 1948, that England was planning to approach France and the so-called Benelux countries (Belgium, Netherlands, Luxembourg) with a proposal for a series of bilateral defence agreements. The pattern he had

[1] Incidentally the decision to incorporate Western Germany in C.E.E.C.'s plans confirmed the *de facto* position of Germany.

[2] Without any overt United States participation, though Clayton, Douglas and Caffery were in the wings to say what Congress would not stand—e.g. to scale down the total from $29 billion over four years to $22·4 (cut by the Harriman Committee to $17 billion) and add pledges to balance budgets.

in mind was that of the Dunkirk Treaty, a post-war agreement by which Great Britain and France had agreed to come to each other's defence in case of renewed German aggression.

General Marshall brought Bevin's message to me. I thought it was a good beginning—a step in the right direction. If the countries of Western Europe were ready to organize for their joint defence, that would be an important contribution to the peace of the world.

Bevin in his message had asked what our attitude would be toward this new alliance. I authorized Marshall to inform the British Foreign Secretary that we agreed with them on the urgent need for concerted measures by the nations of Western Europe. As in the case of the European Recovery Programme, we welcomed European initiative and would give their undertaking our whole-hearted sympathy; the United States would do anything it properly could to assist the European nations to bring this or a similar project to fulfilment.

With this backing from the United States, Bevin approached the French and the Benelux countries."[1]

On 22 January Bevin expounded his plan to the House of Commons: "I believe the time is ripe for a consolidation of Western Europe." He talked about "Western Union" and said, vaguely, it "must primarily be a fusion derived from the basic freedoms and ethical principles for which we all stand . . . It is more of a brotherhood and less of a system." What emerged, in the form of the Brussels Treaty signed on 17 March, 1948, was a good deal less than any union. Although the preamble talked about strengthening "the economic, social and cultural ties" of the signatories, the heart of the Treaty was in the pledge to afford "all military and other aid and assistance in their power" to any one of them which might be attacked. It was essentially military; the signatories were the United Kingdom, France, Holland, Belgium and Luxembourg.

Even before the Treaty was signed there was an ominous development. On 24 February the Communist coup occurred in Prague. On 26 February Britain, the United States and France launched a joint protest against the U.S.S.R.—a step without precedent. On 5 March General Clay, United States military governor in Ger-

[1] Truman, op. cit., Vol. II (New York, 1956), p. 243; (London, 1956), p. 257.

many, warned Washington that tension had reached a point at which war might "come with dramatic suddenness". A few days later (12 March) Bevin made what appears to be the first explicit suggestion of a North Atlantic Pact. Forrestal reports Marshall as having told him that "Bevin makes three proposals:

1. Build around the 5-nation . . . pact.
2. A plan for Atlantic security.
3. A Mediterranean system of security.

Bevin suggests a meeting in Washington between British and American representatives early next week".[1] The Brussels Pact, in other words, had in fact already been recognized to be insufficient, in face of a "clear and present danger". Immediately, all the United States could offer was Mr. Truman's call to Congress on 17 March for Universal Military Training and Selective Service and his reference to the Brussels Treaty as "deserving our full support". On 23 April Bevin argued further for his Atlantic Treaty with United States membership on the grounds that only so could the Russians be deterred from war and only so could the French agree to a rebuilding of Germany. "He expressed the opinion that it would be very difficult for the British, or other free nations, to stand up to new acts of aggression unless there was a definitely worked-out arrangement, which included the United States, for collective resistance against aggression."[2]

There was here some juggling for position. Europe (including not least Great Britain) was very anxious not to launch an Atlantic Pact which the U.S.S.R. would regard as hostile before they had the firm promise of 100 per cent United States support; the United States was very anxious (partly for Congressional reasons) to use the E.R.P. analogy—Europe "to display energy and competence in the perfection of their own plans . . . before we give them any indication of the scope or degree of our support".[3] The argument and the manoeuvring went on throughout the summer, Forrestal recording as late as 12 November:

[1] *The Forrestal Diaries* (New York, 1951), p. 392; (London, 1952), p. 372.

[2] Truman, op. cit., Vol. II (New York), p. 245; (London), pp. 258–9.

[3] *The Forrestal Diaries* (New York), p. 434; (London), p. 409.

D   49

"On the question of an Atlantic Pact, the British [Chiefs of Staff] made it very clear that they considered it essential that the United States should sign a pact to support the Western European powers in the event of 'hostilities'. They were asked what the effect would be if the United States failed to sign a pact but made substantial military shipments; they were unanimous in replying that this would be better than nothing but still 'totally inadequate'."[1]

As far as the United Kingdom was concerned two points lay behind all this:

1. Britain's desire as a European power to get the United States as far into a European commitment as possible, because of her conviction that American support was essential for European defence.
2. Her determination as an insular power with wide extra-European responsibilities not to accept any greater commitment on the continent of Europe than the United States would.

How far, in pursuit of the first aim, the United Kingdom would go, was strikingly demonstrated in June–July, 1948, at the height of the Berlin crisis, when the British were sounded out on whether they would accept two squadrons of B-29s stationed in England and the Foreign Office's reaction, "somewhat to the surprise of the Americans", was "prompt and in the affirmative".[2] There was nothing in the British response that should have surprised anyone. Already in the earlier part of 1947 the Royal Air Force and the U.S. Strategic Air Command had agreed on a long-range flight training programme; not surprisingly therefore, agreement on the stationing of the B-29s had already been reached at the operational level before the diplomats and politicians endorsed it. The decision to accept the atomic bombers, crucial though it was, was in fact in direct line with the kind of responsibilities Britain had already assumed and the kind of relationship with the United States which she had all along been seeking.

Though presented publicly as a temporary arrangement, it is doubtful whether anyone really so regarded it or, if they did, that they imagined that this subtracted from the significance of the

[1] Ibid. (New York), p. 525; (London), p. 490.

[2] Ibid. (New York), pp. 454–5; (London), pp. 427–8.

decision. In August, 1948, another thirty B-29s joined the initial sixty and by the end of the year the number of American air force personnel in Britain had risen to 6,000. When Sir Stafford Cripps, as Chancellor of the Exchequer, visited Washington in October he told Forrestal that "Britain must be regarded as the main base for the deployment of American power and the chief offensive against Russia must be by air".[1] Thus, in advance of agreement on the North Atlantic Treaty, Britain had committed herself to an alliance in arms with the United States and had built her defence strategy around the American atomic deterrent wielded from bases on British soil. Moreover, this was done without any formal treaty agreement; it was an "arrangement", an "understanding" between the political and service chiefs on each side.

The bilateral relationship thus established in air defence was not suitable for application, simply and directly, to the economic problems of Britain and Europe. Yet one may trace elements of the same way of thinking in Britain's attitude to the evolution of the institutions of the Marshall Plan. Thus in the European Recovery Programme (E.R.P.) Britain had thrown her weight in favour of each recipient country negotiating a bilateral treaty with Washington, rather than fusing their negotiating personalities into one and concluding a single multilateral treaty with the United States. On this she got her way. Similarly when the French "Europeanists" had pressed for a strong international secretariat under a powerful chairman for the Organization for European Economic Co-operation (O.E.E.C.) which would develop a vigorous personality of its own and, as such, negotiate directly with member Governments— the kind of structure which had served the European Coal Community—Britain opposed it. Instead she advocated the establishment of sixteen national delegations at Paris, served by a small secretariat in a subordinate role—a kind of continuous international conference. Substantially this was what emerged and, fortuitously in fact, but consequentially as it appeared, the eminent British chairman of the C.E.E.C., Sir Oliver Franks, was not made available to its successor organization, O.E.E.C., but instead was dispatched to Washington as British Ambassador. That no slight to the new organization was intended ought to have been apparent by the selection of Sir Edmund Hall-Patch to be Chairman of the Executive Committee, who made a signal contribution to the sense

[1] Ibid. (New York), p. 491; (London), p. 460.

of European loyalty that became O.E.E.C.'s hall-mark. To the Americans, however, it is doubtful if it appeared that way, especially since Mr. Truman had released his own Secretary of Commerce, Mr. Harriman, to be the American opposite number in Paris. Finally, in line with these restrictions on supra-nationalism and this determination to keep open direct lines of communication with Washington—indeed to give priority to them—was the British desire to see the crucial question of the allocation of funds handled in Washington and not in Paris. Here Britain's main critics were the Americans themselves, who, pressing for European unification, suddenly insisted on the Europeans doing their own shareout, at least to the extent of making their own recommendations for the division of aid. In fact the task proved too much for so large a membership and a Committee of "Four Wise Men"[1] were given the task of making recommendations which the council substantially accepted. In fact also O.E.E.C. recommendations were *only* recommendations. The Economic Cooperation Administration, E.C.A. in Washington always retained the legal power to determine the size of aid allotments and when the aid total was cut at the end of the first two years E.C.A. assumed the major responsibility for fixing the allocation.

As the structure of N.A.T.O. developed, British attitudes towards it could be seen to parallel closely previous attitudes to the Marshall Plan. There was the same aversion to anything suggestive of a supra-national secretariat, though a comparable willingness to second an eminent English public servant, in this case Lord Ismay, and to allow him to develop an "international personality". In the matter of the allocation of American aid there was indeed little question of choice between the bilateral and the multilateral approach. When merely economic aid stopped and the new Mutual Defence Assistance Programme, part economic but mainly military, took its place, the United States naturally preferred to decide itself who should have how much. To Britain, reasonably confident of her ability to demonstrate that she was a good risk and no mere crutch-lover, this arrangement was preferable to any round-table haggling. (N.A.T.O. haggling, as in the Annual Review and over the costs of the infrastructure, proved to be arduous indeed.) Similarly, in strategic planning, the structure of N.A.T.O., with its location of the Standing Group in Washington, was highly accept-

[1] From Italy, France, Belgium and the United Kingdom.

able.[1] Save for the addition of France, was this not the old Combined Chiefs of Staff Committee of World War II, which also had met in Washington? The resemblance of S.H.A.P.E. to S.H.A.E.F. was even more obvious, while the selection of General Eisenhower as Supreme Commander put the organization of European defence into trusted and familiar hands.

Most important of all perhaps, the essential power structure of N.A.T.O. was (indeed still is) that of an alliance in which two members, the United States and Britain, disposed of a strength different not merely in degree but also in kind from that which the rest could command, namely the nuclear deterrent. The British share in this antedated her development of an independent deterrent of her own (if indeed the V-bomber force can properly be so described); it derived essentially from the facilities which as "the unsinkable aircraft carrier" she afforded to U.S. Strategic Air Command (S.A.C.) at a time when other bases were, in varying degrees, impracticable because they were either liable to be overrun by Soviet ground forces or were only leaseable from politically unstable ground landlords. But all along S.A.C. has remained outside N.A.T.O., an arm exclusively and directly under U.S. control. There was thus a paradox at the heart of N.A.T.O. (and still is), that as an alliance it never controlled forces adequate for the defence of its members; owing to the persistent failure in the build-up of its ground troops, it depended always upon the two air forces which it did not control, S.A.C. and Bomber Command. That this was an element of weakness, and that it occasioned jealousies and anxieties amongst the members is almost certainly true, but from the British point of view this feature of N.A.T.O. was not the least of its recommendations. A N.A.T.O. which sought to oppose the Soviet millions by an equivalent build-up of ground forces would have drained Britain dry of man-power and left her nothing with which to deal with the "limited" and "brush-fire" wars which might come her way as a worldwide power. It would also have put Britain very much on a par with all the continental European members, with so much of a voice (and no more) as the numbers of her armed forces would have entitled her to. The balance maintained

[1] The Standing Group's prestige declined from 1953 onwards, when the Chairman of the United States Chiefs of Staff ceased to be the day-to-day American representative on the Group; in his place came another senior officer.

between the conventional forces of N.A.T.O. and the nuclear deterrent was essentially what enabled Britain to continue operating in her dual capacity as a European and an Atlantic power. Moreover, it enabled her to build and maintain the Anglo-American alliance within a structure of Western European collective security, thus by-passing many, if not all, the problems that an exclusively bilateral arrangement would have created, both in Europe and in America. Finally it put her on a par with the United States in respect of an issue on which she was peculiarly sensitive—her degree of insularity or commitment. She was able to hold to her contention that as an island power with worldwide obligations she was as good a European as that quasi-island power with worldwide commitments, the United States, and that she would go into Europe as far as America would go (even if that involved greater risks for her than for America, as a more vulnerable and contiguous country) but that she was not under any obligation to go farther.

The testing time for "thus far and no farther" came very soon after the N.A.T.O. structure had been built. When the Korean War made vivid the menace of Communism on the march and at the same time diverted much American strength towards the Pacific, the inadequacy of N.A.T.O.s forces became glaringly apparent. The demand for the creation of a German army to help in the manning of the European ramparts grew proportionally. It did not indeed grow at an equal pace in Britain and America. Britain, to some extent, had her hand forced by American pressure. Left to herself, she would certainly have preferred to wait rather than demand from a defeated enemy a contribution to an anti-Russian defence force. Britain was more reluctant than the U.S.A. to believe that Germany's "re-education" in democracy and non-aggression was complete at the end of a five-year course. She was also more willing to credit the Soviet argument that once West Germany was re-armed the reunification of Germany would be out of the question. These differences apart, no one disputed that the revival of a German instrument of war would be only tolerable to her old enemies and victims if it were integrated in a larger whole which it could never hope to dominate. Thus arose the idea of a European army, to which indeed even so robust a British patriot as Winston Churchill gave his endorsement at the Council of Europe in August, 1950. What perhaps his auditors failed to notice was his proviso that such a force should act "in full co-operation with

54

the United States and Canada". Even so, it was a misleading index of Britain's own intentions. The Americans, announcing that they would send more troops to Europe (Mr. Truman on 5 September, 1950), began also to step up their pressure for German rearmament. The French, hating the idea of a German national army, hastily devised the Pleven Plan (national contingents integrated at the level of the smallest possible unit under a European Defence Minister, responsible to the European Assembly with a European budget and Defence Council). But when it came to working out details in the first half of 1951, the United Kingdom made it clear that it would not join the European Army and to the meeting held at Paris to discuss the Plan in February, 1951, Britain sent only an observer. However, when it became apparent later in the year that a direct German contribution to N.A.T.O. would not be acceptable and that the European Defence Community (E.D.C.) was the only alternative, the United Kingdom joined with the United States and France in giving it support. Herbert Morrison, as Foreign Secretary, said we desired to establish "the closest possible association" with it "at all stages of its development". The statement was, however, more indicative of the ambivalence of British pronouncements than of any change of policy.

If, when Mr. Churchill took over from Mr. Attlee in October, 1951, the Europeans expected the great proponent of a European Army to lead the United Kingdom into E.D.C., they were quickly disillusioned. Despite keen and constant American pressure the response of the British Government was cool. Sir David Maxwell-Fyfe was sent to Strasbourg to say that Britain would "consider" the best way of "associating" herself with a European army—a far cry from integrating her forces in one. In other words the British Government was for a European army—but from outside; Britain was to be a well-wisher, not a participant. We have Sir Anthony Eden's word for it[1] that this policy enjoyed, from November, 1951, onwards, official American support (though he admits even "well-informed" Americans still blamed us for not going in). He does not say what considerations led to this change in the American attitude but to the extent to which it took place it was certainly welcome in Britain. As the E.D.C. negotiations proceeded it became more and more apparent that the British relationship with any such defence community would not be any more intimate than the

[1] A. Eden, *Full Circle* (London, Boston, 1960), pp. 32–36.

American. In pursuance of this policy it was a joint and identical assurance that Britain and the U.S.A. gave on the morrow of the signing of the E.D.C. Treaty that

> "If any action from whatever quarter threatens the integrity or unity of the Community, the two Governments will regard this as a threat to their own security. They will act in accordance with Article 4 of the North Atlantic Treaty."

In fact, of course, this assurance was not enough to secure the ratification of the E.D.C. Treaty. For nearly two years the E.D.C. debate dragged on inconclusively in France. In face of this, American impatience and irritation mounted. In October, 1953, Dulles as U.S. Secretary of State threatened France with his "agonizing reappraisal" and the threat that Congress might not continue to support N.A.T.O. Aimed primarily at France it also had its implications for Britain. This was the time when Dulles informed Eden that

> "If things went wrong the United States might swing over to a policy of western hemispheric defence, with emphasis on the Far East. . . . Mr. Dulles pointed out that the consequences of a swing of American policy towards hemispheric defence were of obvious concern to Great Britain. He hoped therefore that they might find an occasion to underline the warnings which he had issued in his statement and make some appeal to France."[1]

In August, 1954, nonetheless, the French Assembly rejected E.D.C. The situation thus precipitated was far more critical than any that had existed before E.D.C. had been thought of. To resolve this *crise de confiance*, even though in the strict sense it was none of her making, and to make possible the only other conceivable solution, the admission of Germany into N.A.T.O., Britain gave a pledge "to maintain on the mainland of Europe . . . the effective strength of the United Kingdom forces now assigned to S.A.C.E.U.R., four divisions and the Tactical Air Force, or whatever S.A.C.E.U.R. regards as equivalent fighting capacity" and not to withdraw them against the wishes of a majority of the Brussels Powers. For the United States Dulles also gave an undertaking but it was in a less explicit form—the United States "to maintain in Europe . . . such units . . . as may be necessary and appropriate to contribute its fair

[1] Ibid., pp. 57–58.

share of the forces needed . . . etc." In retrospect the discrepancy between the two commitments may not appear unduly significant; if so, it is because the British Government has not allowed the Paris Agreements to set a precedent in creating such discrepancies—indeed, as the British Defence White Paper of 1957 soon showed, it has not interpreted the Agreements themselves as constituting quite as rigid a commitment as at first appeared.

5

THE ATOM

WITH the establishment of N.A.T.O. and the creation of the working partnership in the nuclear deterrent there came into being again an informal Anglo-American alliance which, *mutatis mutandis*, incorporated most of the essential features of the wartime relationship. There was, however, one area of activity which was conspicuously excluded from the Anglo-American partnership. Anything to do with the great discovery with which the war ended, the management of the annihilating energies of the atom, remained a jealously guarded national secret. The story, fragmentary and at many points obscure, thanks to the technical complexity of the subject matter and the enveloping curtain of official secrecy, begins with the outbreak of the war itself.

Anglo-American co-operation in the field of government-sponsored scientific research may be said to date from the dispatch to America of Sir Henry Tizard's mission in August, 1940. In Tizard's own words the policy behind his mission was simply "to tell them what they want to know".[1] The Americans were deeply impressed by such openness and reciprocated with an equal generosity. By the beginning of 1941 the British Government had committed itself to an explicit policy of disclosing all scientific and technical secrets to the Americans, withholding only those which might involve the security of imminent operations or where the developments being explored were still immature. This applied, by no means least, to British researches on what was then known as the U-bomb;[2] in October, 1941, while the U.S.A. was still at peace, Roosevelt suggested to Churchill that work on this project should be conducted jointly. The suggestion was not adopted in that form, but from the autumn of 1941 to the autumn of 1942 frequent visits and constant exchanges of papers established a virtual pooling of British and American findings. By June, 1942, it seemed to have become possible—and if possible then indeed imperative—to proceed from

[1] H. Duncan Hall and C. C. Wrigley, *Studies of Overseas Supply*, pp. 361, 368.

[2] Its code name until November, 1941, was *Maud*, and after that date *Tube Alloys*.

research to production and in a striking passage in his *Second World War* Sir Winston Churchill describes how he and President Roosevelt, sitting in "intense heat" in a "tiny little room" at Hyde Park agreed to abandon work in Britain, and, in the interests of economy and security, concentrate research and production in the United States.

"I strongly urged that we should at once pool all our information, work together on equal terms, and share the results, if any, equally between us. The question then arose as to where the research plant was to be set up. We were already aware of the enormous expense that must be incurred, with all the consequent grave diversion of resources and brain-power from other forms of war-effort. Considering that Great Britain was under close bombing attack and constant enemy air reconnaissance, it seemed impossible to erect in the island the vast and conspicuous factories that were needed. We conceived ourselves at least as far advanced as our Ally, and there was of course the alternative of Canada, who had a vital contribution herself to make through the supplies of uranium she had actively gathered. It was a hard decision to spend several hundred million pounds sterling, not so much of money as of competing forms of precious war energy, upon a project the success of which no scientist on either side of the Atlantic could guarantee. Nevertheless, if the Americans had not been willing to undertake the venture we should certainly have gone forward on our own power in Canada, or, if the Canadian Government demurred, in some other part of the Empire. I was, however, very glad when the President said he thought the United States would have to do it. We therefore took this decision jointly, and settled a basis of agreement."[1]

However, of this momentous agreement no written record was made and by the time subordinates came to translate the generalities of their masters into specific directives, the American programme had entered a new phase. In August, 1942, when the project was ripe for transfer from laboratory to factory, the U.S. Army Corps of Engineers assumed control of what their code called the "Manhattan District" and in so doing brought in with them a military concept of security. The signature in September of the Anglo-Russian agreement for the exchange of weapons seems to have been

[1] Churchill, *The Second World War*, Vol. IV, (London) pp. 341–2, (New York) pp. 380–1.

another inhibiting factor for the American administration.[1] Soon a new doctrine evolved in American scientific-military thinking, that no information should be exchanged even with their closest allies beyond what would directly benefit the war effort. As, in the interests of security, work on the bomb became increasingly compartmentalized, so the number and importance of the compartments to which the British were given access declined. By the end of 1942 there was a virtual cessation of all flow of information to the British.

In January, 1943, Churchill protested about this to Roosevelt at the Casablanca Conference. Receiving hearty assurances but no action from the President, Churchill pressed his case with Harry Hopkins, warning him that if the Americans were not more forthcoming Britain would be compelled to go ahead separately.[2] In May at Washington Churchill secured Roosevelt's agreement "that the exchange of information on tube alloys should be resumed, and that the enterprise should be considered a joint one", and at their Quebec meeting in August, 1943, a specific document incorporating these principles was drawn up.[3]

Under the Quebec Agreement a Combined Policy Committee was established consisting of three Americans, two British and one Canadian member to oversee the project and provide a channel through which information could be exchanged. The clauses which dealt with the exchange of information were, as Lord Attlee later remarked, "loosely worded"; the first spoke of "complete interchange of information and ideas on all sections of the project", another stipulated that "in the field of design, construction and operation of large-scale plants" interchange would be regulated by "such *ad hoc* arrangements as may, in each section of the field, appear to be necessary or desirable if the project is to be brought to fruition at the earliest moment. Such *ad hoc* arrangements shall be subject to the approval of the Policy Committee".

[1] R. G. Hewlett and O. E. Anderson, *History of the U.S. Atomic Energy Commission*, Vol. I, pp. 267–8.

[2] R. Sherwood, *Roosevelt and Hopkins,* pp. 700–1.

[3] Churchill, *The Second World War*, Vol. IV, (London) p. 723, (New York) p. 809, telegram to Sir John Anderson, and Vol. V, (London) p. 83, (New York) p. 93 telegram to Deputy Prime Minister and War Cabinet.

Of a rather different order were four politico-economic clauses of the agreement; these were mutual undertakings "that we will never use this agency against each other", "that we will not use it against third parties without each other's consent" and "that we will not communicate any information . . . to third parties except by mutual consent"; finally, in order to quiet the American suspicions that the British were primarily interested in securing information which would give them a commercial advantage after the war, the following clause was added: "In view of the heavy burden of production falling upon the United States as a result of a wise division of war effort, the British Government recognize that any post-war advantages of an industrial or commercial character shall be dealt with as between the United States and Great Britain on terms to be specified by the President of the United States to the Prime Minister of Great Britain. The Prime Minister expressly disclaims any interest in these industrial and commercial aspects beyond what may be considered by the President of the United States to be fair and just and in harmony with the economic welfare of the world."[1]

The Quebec Agreement was secret, so secret that in Britain even the War Cabinet was not informed of its provisions. Mr. Attlee learnt them for the first time only when he took over as Premier in 1945; so, presumably, did Mr. Truman in the same way. According to Senator McMahon, neither he nor any of his Congressional colleagues knew of them until 1947. In retrospect this appears a grave error. Dr. Conant, who had a major role in drafting the Agreement and was a founder member of the Combined Policy Committee, gave it as his opinion in 1952 that

"if at least a committee of the Senate of the United States had been apprised of the United States-British war-time negotiations when they took place, the Bill that set up the Atomic Energy Commission of the United States might have taken a different form and Anglo-American relations after a rough passage might be better now. As a very humble observer from a distance of what occurred at high levels in 1943, I thought then and I still think that a treaty should have been drawn between the three nations involved, a treaty dealing with everything even distinctly related to atomic energy. I for one certainly regret the existence of barriers to full Anglo-American co-operation in all aspects of

[1] Command Paper 9123, 6 April, 1954.

applied nuclear physics, yet the events of the last few years have made the removal of these barriers difficult, to say the least."[1]

The Quebec Agreement, even during the war, did not work without some creaking. General Groves, head of the Manhattan Project, never believed in interchange and, on his own proud admission, worked against it.[2] Nevertheless the Agreement served as the basis for British participation in the later stages of the work on the bomb and in general co-operation was good. Moreover, in June, 1944, the Combined Policy Committee was supplemented by a Combined Development Trust. This, financed jointly by Britain and the United States, was established to buy up and control all available supplies of uranium and thorium ores.

By September, 1944, the time was ripe for thinking about the possible post-war implications of atomic energy. Visiting Roosevelt then, after the second Quebec Conference, Churchill agreed with him on an *aide-mémoire* which looked beyond the terms of the Quebec Agreement; this document stated that "full collaboration between the United States and the British Government in developing Tube Alloys for military and commercial purposes should continue after the defeat of Japan unless terminated by joint agreement".[3] More confidential even than the Quebec Agreement, the *aide-mémoire* was not even disclosed by Roosevelt at the time to his closest "Tube Alloys" adviser, Henry Stimson, and the only American copy of it was lost in an irrelevant file for years. Though its intent was clear, its exact legal status became debatable once Roosevelt's death and Churchill's resignation removed its two signatories from power.

When the bomb came alive in all its horrifying actuality at Hiroshima and Nagasaki two considerations were uppermost in the thinking of Mr. Attlee's Government. The first was the need, if possible, to establish some effective international control of the new scientific monster. The second was the need to consolidate and extend the existing arrangements for Anglo-American partnership in the atomic field. In the eyes of the British Government the two objectives were not thought to be incompatible. The Americans, or

[1] J. B. Conant, *Anglo-American Relations in the Atomic Age*, p. 33.

[2] U.S. Atomic Energy Commission, In the Matter of J. Robert Oppenheimer (Washington 1954), pp. 174–5, 177.

[3] Hewlett and Anderson, op. cit., p. 327 and pp. 457–8.

many of them at any rate, were not so sure. Three schools could be discerned; the out-and-out internationalists; the Anglo-Americanists; and those who believed that the "secrets" of the bomb could and should be kept by the United States. In the mind of Mr. Truman, new to his fearful responsibilities, elements of all three attitudes seem to have co-existed. Mr. Attlee's desire for an early meeting to hammer out a joint approach to the problems of the bomb derived urgency in October, 1945, from the President's remarks at a press conference that the United States would not share the "know-how" of the bomb's manufacture with its allies. The meeting, at which Mackenzie King also participated, for Canada, took place in Washington in November.

No detailed report of the meeting has been published, but from the fullest account available[1] it would appear that the main item of the agenda was the international control of atomic energy and that it was not until late in the meetings that the future of Anglo-American co-operation was considered; it was then entrusted by the principals to their subordinates, working wearily against time. What came out was the "Agreed Declaration" of 16 November which advocated international action to control atomic energy and to outlaw weapons of mass destruction, with effective safeguards through inspection. To this was appended a memorandum that read as follows:

"1. We desire that there should be full and effective co-operation in the field of atomic energy between the United States, the United Kingdom and Canada.

2. We agree that the Combined Policy Committee and the Combined Development Trust should be continued in a suitable form.

3. We request the Combined Policy Committee to consider and recommend to us appropriate arrangements for this purpose."

Lord Attlee says he and Sir John Anderson came away from the talks thinking they had obtained "a satisfactory agreement for future co-operation in the field of atomic energy". No reference was made in the communiqué to the Quebec Agreement, least of all to the politico-economic clauses. This was one of the matters on which the Combined Policy Committee was to make recommendations.

[1] Hewlett and Anderson, op. cit., p. 455–81.

When the Combined Policy Committee got down to this task it found that at the operative level a crucial gap existed between British and American thinking. The British asked for the implementation of the "full and effective co-operation" of the Truman-Attlee-King memorandum. On the American side, however, a paradoxical alliance emerged of the nationalists and the internationalists, General Groves insisting that any such exchange of information with the United Kingdom would compromise the attempts to set up international control of the bomb through the United Nations. As a result nearly six months went by without any progress at all. To make matters worse, the American administration was lending its support in Congress to the McMahon Bill which proposed a number of sweeping restrictions on the disclosure or exchange of information in the atomic energy field, reflecting the pervasive Congressional conviction that the U.S.A. had the "secret" of the atom bomb and that she ought to preserve this in her exclusive possession even from her closest allies.

In face of this Mr. Attlee "informed the United States ambassador in London, Mr. Harriman, that if the McMahon Bill was passed Britain would be forced to build her own plants for atomic energy production for both military and civil purposes. At the same time he instructed Lord Halifax in Washington to request detailed information on the construction and operation of atomic energy plants in the United States at the next meeting of the Combined Policy Committee in order that Britain should have the necessary data to complete the work. The request was put at a meeting on 15 April. It met with a blank refusal".[1]

There then ensued a sharply worded exchange of notes between the two leaders, an outline of which may be read in Mr. Truman's *Memoirs* and Lord Attlee's recorded reminiscences, *A Prime Minister Remembers*. For Britain, of course, there were two aspects to the problem, both of which appeared equally important in the context of conditions in 1946. Not only was there the obvious desire to share in the super-weapon, but also, with British coal production lagging and oil constituting a large element in our import bill, the atom as a source of fuel and power had a special appeal, all the greater since somewhat optimistic estimates prevailed about the cheapness of atomic power. In pressing their case the United Kingdom relied mainly on the "complete interchange" clause of the

[1] Francis Williams, *A Prime Minister Remembers* (1961), p. 110.

Quebec Agreement plus the moral argument of the United Kingdom's contribution to the wartime project; the United States in rebuttal contended that Quebec was never meant to cover plant construction and also that while a plan for the international control of atomic energy was before the United Nations any exclusive exchange between the United Kingdom and the United States would be improper.

The Attlee-Truman exchanges were still in progress on 1 August, 1946, when the McMahon Bill became law. No reply was ever received in Britain to Mr. Attlee's last and fullest exposition of the British claims and no doubt any reply from the American administration would have had only academic interest since, with the enactment of the Bill, an immediate ban was placed on all conveyance of information. Already in January, 1946, the Government had announced the establishment of an organization in the Ministry of Supply which would "be responsible for the production of fissile material" and would develop the atomic energy programme "as circumstances may require", i.e. to make both atomic power and atomic bombs.[1] The imposition of the American ban meant that there could be no more hope of division of labour or sharing of expense in the development programme. The Government had now only the choice of turning back or accelerating and expanding the work it had begun. It chose the latter. As soon as Parliament reassembled in October the House of Commons gave a second reading to the Atomic Energy Bill which gave the Ministry of Supply a monopoly in the atomic energy field, with full powers of development and control.

In 1947, in late spring or early summer, certain key Republican Senators, notably Senator Hickenlooper, chairman of the Atomic Energy Commission, and Senator Vandenberg, chairman of the Foreign Relations Committee, learnt of the political clauses of the Quebec agreement and immediately pressed for their elimination. They also objected to the fact that the original uranium agreements, made in 1944, by which all uranium that the three countries could obtain (including the Congo supplies) was turned over to the United States, had been modified in July, 1946, to provide for an approximate equal division between the United Kingdom and the United States. Vandenberg said he thought the Hyde Park and Quebec arrangements "astounding" and "unthinkable" and said

[1] H. C. Deb., 5th series, Vol. 418, col. 682-3.

that "failure to revamp the agreements would have a disastrous effect on Congressional consideration of the Marshall Plan . . . a satisfactory conclusion must be reached before final action on the Marshall Plan programme".[1] As a result, on 8 January, 1948, agreement was reached—(the so called *modus vivendi*)

(*a*) to remove restrictions on the use of the bomb (though it is generally accepted that Mr. Truman gave a personal pledge that the United States would continue to work in the spirit of Quebec);

(*b*) to give the United States more ore; e.g. all the Congo uranium produced in 1948–9 to go to the United States and the United States to be given additional allocations from the British owned stockpile if these were needed to maintain the minimum American programme;

(*c*) in return, the United States to disclose to the United Kingdom nuclear data in nine "areas of information having to do with health and safety and certain other things", within the limits of the McMahon Act, military information specifically excluded.

The *modus vivendi* was to run only to December, 1949, and Mr. Truman, in considering its renewal, proposed in July, 1949, to Congressional leaders, especially Hickenlooper and Vandenberg, what would in effect have been something of a revival of the wartime intimacy. (The limited evidence suggests that the British were insisting that a full partnership was required by the world situation.) Mr. Truman, reviving the argument of Britain's wartime contribution to the bomb, proposed: "a full partnership, subject to the terms of the Atomic Energy Act"; all available uranium to be brought to the United States for processing and storage; British and Canadian scientists to come to the United States to work with their American colleagues; "to overcome any complaints the British might have that they were being excluded from the atomic weapons field, we could arrange to have a number of our un-assembled bombs placed in the British Isles".[2]

[1] *The Papers of Senator Vandenberg* (Boston, 1952; London, 1953), p. 361.

[2] Truman, op. cit., Vol. II (New York), pp. 303–4; (London), pp. 320–1.

There is, so far as I know, no published evidence as to whether or not these proposals had the support of the British Government. They represented, in effect, a re-creation of the wartime project, including the siting of the whole operation in the United States. Anxious as Britain was to receive access to all information, it is possible that she would not have been eager, in 1949, to buy it at such a price; moreover, the wartime precedent was a good deal less happy in the atomic field than in others. In any event the proposal came to nothing. Senator Vandenberg opposed it, as his biographer states, on the remarkable grounds that "the United States had . . . continuously extended its aid to Britain and without any overwhelming co-operation in return", that the Atlantic Pact implied defence specialization, and that the United States was particularly equipped to carry the prime responsibility in the nuclear field. Senator Hickenlooper also objected on the ground of "his distrust of British security".[1] In August, 1949, the American monopoly— or, one should more truly say, their imagined monopoly—of A-bomb secrets was in fact brought to an end—but by another rival than her ally. In September it was established beyond doubt that the Russians, a month earlier, had exploded an atomic "device".

At the end of 1949 the *modus vivendi* did run out and even the limited exchange possible under it ceased to operate. In the new year the British Government seems to have submitted new proposals, but on 4 February Dr. Klaus Fuchs was prosecuted in Britain for offences against the Official Secrets Act. In the next month Senator McCarthy made public his allegation about Communists in the State Department. On 1 March it was announced that talks which had been taking place in Washington about co-operation in the atomic field would be discontinued pending a review by the three countries concerned of all aspects of their security arrangements. Thus the arrangements in the *modus vivendi* came formally to an end. Contacts indeed continued on an informal basis, but there was no increase in the exchange of information on the existing restricted level.

This frozen posture persisted throughout the remainder of the Attlee and Truman régimes. The resolute American refusal to admit her partner in World War II and now her closest ally in N.A.T.O. to any share in the secrets, military or industrial, of the invention to which British effort had so signally contributed was

[1] Vandenberg, op. cit., p. 364.

undoubtedly the biggest flaw, from the British point of view, in the Anglo-American partnership during these years. The peculiarly charged quality of the subject, coupled with its technical obscurity, damped down public discussion of it to a deceptively low level. The desire to move the American Congress and administration by an open appeal to what were felt to be their moral obligations, strove unsuccessfully with the dominant disposition to go easy on public protests so long as there was a reasonable prospect that private representations, particularly at the executive level, might modify statutory vetoes. But the pent-up frustration thus engendered occasionally found outlet in explosions of ill-temper in Parliament in which political leaders, unable to give frank expression to their irritation with their allies, vented their feelings upon the opposite front-bench. The deep sense of mortification and injustice which rankled on this subject can be detected in the intermittent and often oblique exchanges during this period between Churchill and Attlee and their respective lieutenants. At the always silent level of official Whitehall not even these bubbles of exasperation rose to the surface, but it was perhaps in Whitehall more than anywhere else that this breakdown of a looked-for co-operation became a souring element in a relationship otherwise harmonious and mutually esteemed.

There is every indication that Mr. Churchill confidently looked for a change on this front as a result of his return to power and his Washington visit of January, 1952. Since 1948 the British case, in his view, had been powerfully reinforced by the acceptance of East Anglia of those S.A.C. bomber bases which, being as it were the spring boards of American atomic might, exposed Britain to a peculiar hazard of atomic attack. But this, though it might be a valid debating-point, was not a bargaining counter, since no one save British isolationists or fellow-travellers really wished to see the Americans expelled from these bases and British atomic bombs and bombers replace American ones. In fact Mr. Churchill was no more effective in his pleas for a resumption of sharing than Attlee had been. He obtained the limited, and indeed debatable, advantage of getting in writing the hitherto informal agreement that the atom bomb should not be loosed from American bases in East Anglia without British consent. But on the information front, he obtained nothing. Finally on 3 October, 1952, the United Kingdom exploded her own atom bomb on the Montebello Islands. How much it cost, how much more it cost as a result of Britain having to "go it alone"—no meaningful answers to these questions have ever been published. Mr. Churchill, on various occasions, spoke of "many scores of millions of pounds" and of "well over £100 million". Such estimates certainly do not err on the side of overstatement, but no official figures have ever been released.

The eventual acquisition by Britain, through her own efforts, of the "secret" of the atom bomb was, of course, by the strange logic which governed American policy on this subject, the most powerful argument for the readmission of Britain to the atomic partnership. But about the same time other factors began to operate to produce a certain modification of American policy. The Eisenhower Administration which took over in 1953 enjoyed a somewhat greater prestige amongst secrecy-minded Congressmen than its predecessor; this coincided with the need to make some response to the worldwide shock produced by hydrogen bomb explosion at Eniwetok and a growing realization of the need to apprise America's allies of the military implications of atomic weapons. The decision in September, 1952, to send atomic artillery to American forces in Europe was an important factor in this. And in October, 1953, further successful British atomic test explosions were conducted. Even so it was not until February, 1954, that the President asked Congress to amend the McMahon Act to permit the exchange of information on the tactical uses of atomic energy. At the end of August the President signed amending legislation which pretty well gave him what he asked. It was still less than the British wanted; weapons secrets were still excluded. British expenditure on making her own bombs still ran at a level which the *Manchester Guardian* estimated at more than £100 million a year, and when the British exploded a hydrogen bomb of their own on Christmas Island in 1957 it was still a British made weapon. Still the log-jam had been broken; by degrees further agreements extended the area of co-operation. Most important perhaps of all, the interpretations given to the agreements by officials concerned were genuinely liberal in spirit. The worst of the discriminatory sting was drawn; from the British point of view a notable aberration of alliance policy was on the way to being rectified.

6

THE FAR EAST

THE basic identity of policy and strategy which the United Kingdom developed with the U.S.A. in Europe was not reproduced in the Far East. In the ordinary pattern of British and American thinking about Anglo-American relations the Far East occupied only a marginal place; this somewhat obscured from public notice the full nature and extent of the disagreements which marked their policies in this area. These could be traced back at least as far as the American pressure in the 1920's which brought to an end the Anglo-Japanese Alliance. This was followed by the ragged controversy between Sir John Simon and Mr. Henry Stimson over how to deal with the Japanese aggression in Manchuria in 1931. As war in Europe approached, something akin to a surrender of British interests in the Far East developed, with the U.S.A. making what pace there was in the race against Japan for local control. But once the conflict in Europe was joined, the Pacific in British eyes became an ocean of menace for a different reason—the fear that concern for American interests there would draw American aid (and after Pearl Harbour, men and arms) away from Europe to Asia. "Pacific Firstism" was the great British bogey of World War II; in British eyes American leaders were marked up or down in proportion as they resisted or succumbed to this heresy. Inevitably, in a war which began with a Japanese attack on Hawaii and which involved a constant threat to the U.S.A.'s Pacific flank, there was ample scope, even within a surprisingly ready American acceptance of an "Atlantic First" strategy, for a considerable crop of jealousies and squabbles about policies in the Far East. The rapid collapse of Hong Kong, Singapore and Malaya in 1941-2 brought American criticisms of "decadent colonialism".[1] In British eyes Roosevelt's resolute adherence to the pretence that Chiang Kai-shek represented a great power constituted an extraordinary aberration of judgment. But even Americans like Stilwell who did not share this illusion found other grounds for a vinegarish animos-

[1] Cf. as a later by-product of this, Roosevelt's private proposal to Stalin at Yalta that Hong Kong should be given back to the Chinese.

70

ity to the British "presence" in this theatre and his rivalry with Wingate became in British eyes a crime which Hollywood compounded by its demonstration that in fact it was Erroll Flynn who had recaptured Burma. Finally the determination of Admiral King not only, as was natural, to engross for his theatre all the men and material he could divert from anywhere else, but also to resist all control by the Combined Chiefs of Staff and to reject out of hand the British offer in September, 1944, to assist in the central Pacific operations—all this was something which the British found in striking contrast to the basic harmony which prevailed with the U.S.A. in all the other theatres of war.

The explanation of these divergencies was to be found in geography and history. To Britain, the Far East, though of genuine and long-standing interest was, so to say, the last station on the imperial line. Britain had come into Asia by way of India and the Indian Ocean, with Singapore the "gate" to the "Far" East which lay beyond. The area was thus found to have the lowest priority in the British scheme of things; it was, literally, the opposite side of the world, and a side moreover where (unlike the Antipodes) there were no settlements of British blood to beckon across the intervening immensities. For the United States, though ancestry and habit bound her to Europe, the Far East was only a logical extension of that "westward movement" which she had long felt to be her "manifest destiny". The moment she had established herself on the Pacific coast, she had a direct concern for the policing of that ocean and a direct interest in what power dominated even its further shores. Indeed, with the acquisition of Alaska, Hawaii and the Philippines, she became closer to Asia than to Europe.

Out of the facts of geography grew considerations of strategy. The Pacific only comes alive strategically to the United Kingdom when a threat looks like developing there to her communications with Australia and New Zealand. But to Americans it is a Pacific power which comes nearest to their own shores; Asiatic Russia is closer than anywhere in Europe; the Monroe Doctrine, after all, was in part a response to the Tsar's claim to the Pacific litoral as far south as the 51st parallel. The development of modern navies and air forces stimulated the American desire to push her protective bases as far forward as possible, until, with the defeat of Japan in 1945, her strategic frontier ran as far East as a line through the

Aleutians, Japan and the Philippines. Here was the Pacific counter-part to the N.A.T.O. line from Norway to Turkey, the paling within which any adequate containment of Communist power should take place.[1]

The geographical and strategical priorities were reinforced by powerful sentimental ones. The sort of politico-cultural investment which the British felt themselves to have in India, the Americans felt themselves to have in China and, of course, in the Philippines, the legacy in each case of administrators, teachers and missionaries. For the British, the circumstances in which a Labour Government granted independence to India gave Labour almost more than the Conservatives a kind of proprietary sympathy for the newly emergent India of Nehru and guaranteed that a sense of mutual concern would survive the liquidation of British rule. For the Americans the circumstances in which the Kuomintang, enjoying American support, was overthrown in China by a rising tide of Communism made it possible to believe that any Chinese hostility to the U.S.A. was ephemeral or at any rate manufactured. In Japan, of course, the easy assumption by MacArthur of the powers of the Shogunate and the ready acquiescence by the Japanese in the régime of their conquerors invested the American occupation with an air of Platonic "guardianship" which was naturally pleasing to any country with a sense of mission. Small wonder that the American disposition to be exclusive in this role was a powerful one. Though a Far Eastern Commission of eleven nations taking part in the war in the Pacific had been set up in Washington in 1945 and though there was an Allied Council in Tokio with a representative each for the U.S.A., the British Commonwealth, the U.S.S.R. and China, neither body seriously encroached on the American monopoly of administration in post-war Japan.

Thus, though there were certain discrepancies between the British and the American assessments of how a defeated Japan ought to be run, the very exclusiveness of the MacArthur principate prevented this becoming an area of friction. The real disagreement developed over China. Here American policy assumed an almost febrile character which reflected the internal arguments and disputes that had gone into its making and which undoubtedly greatly complicated for

[1] For an incisive analysis of this see G. F. Hudson, *Will Britain and America Split in Asia?* in "Foreign Affairs", June, 1953.

Britain the task of co-ordinating policies with America in the Far East. In 1949 when the Chinese Communists completed their victory by expelling the Kuomintang from mainland China a furious controversy over what was significantly called the "loss" of China broke out both in the American administration and throughout the country. Into the argument about the respective merits of the two Chinese groupings was injected a bitter party feeling derived from the rivalries of the Republicans with a Democratic party which had excluded them from office for almost twenty years. Nothing remotely approaching the bipartisan policy towards Europe existed in respect of the Far East. But although the differences in the debate were real and from the British point of view important, even the Democrats (or most of them) began their argument from a point which was, so to say, a good deal to the right of the British view. Even where the belief in the Kuomintang's virtue had been shattered beyond repair, even where the fact of Communist ascendancy was accepted and outside intervention excluded, there was no abatement in the conviction that the Communist régime was the enemy.

In Britain, on the other hand, for various reasons, a far more indulgent view prevailed. In the absence of any paternalistic fondness for Chiang Kai-shek, the venalities and inadequacies of the Kuomintang had been earlier perceived and more brutally enunciated. This had encouraged an earlier credence for the Chinese Communist claims that they were only a movement of national purification. The image developed of the "People's Republic" as an austere, high-minded, egalitarian society of undernourished peasants whose Marxism was a mere tool for overthrowing age-old superstitions and who only asked to be left alone to build a new China in peace. This pleasing mirage undoubtedly exercised a powerful influence over elements in the post-war Labour Government.

The first open disagreement between London and Washington came over the issue of recognition. Mr. Acheson, as Secretary of State, proposed three tests which the new régime in China would have to pass before the U.S.A. would recognize it. It must be in effective control of the country, it must recognize and carry out its international obligations, it must rule with the acquiescence of the ruled. The moral criteria involved in the second and third of these principles were, of course, such as the government of Mao Tse-tung was ill-equipped to satisfy. The British, here as in general elsewhere, adhered to a morally neutral theory of recognition, that it should be an acknowledgement of fact, not a mark of approbation. But the Acheson test, however open to criticism as importing unassimilable elements into the relations of peaceful states, was in the direct line of earlier, moralistic policies in this same area; it was, after all, in relation to the Japanese conquests in Manchukuo that the Hoover-Stimson doctrine of non-recognition of territories acquired by force had been enunciated. Moreover it was a doctrine which in 1932 the League of Nations Assembly emphatically endorsed at the instance of Sir John Simon. There was, therefore, material here for a fairly charged dispute between the two countries.

We know little about the preliminary discussions between the United Kingdom and the United States on this subject, except that they produced no agreement. The British decision to accord recognition was prompted, it seems fairly clear, by three principal considerations. British commercial interests in China were considerable; in 1950 their value was estimated at £110 million, much greater than those of the United States. In Hong Kong we had another very valuable outpost of trade and investment, highly vulnerable, should China ever decide to move in on it. (On 12 August, 1949, Mr. Acheson had denied that there was any American commitment to defend Hong Kong.) Whatever views one held of the intentions of the Chinese Communist régime there was some reason to suppose that some of its hostility might be drawn by a *de jure* recognition of a rule which *de facto* was certainly absolute, and in some British circles this went so far as to encourage the hope that Mao Tse-tung might be weaned from his dependence on Moscow and become the Tito of the Far East. The error of this hypothesis may now be plain to see but one reason in Britain for embracing it was that it was firmly held in India where Nehru was pressing for early recognition. Undoubtedly the desire to keep in step with the Asiatic parts of the Commonwealth was a powerful factor in accelerating British recognition. Thus Indian recognition was accorded on 30 December, Pakistan's on 4 January, Ceylon's on 6 January and Britain's on the same day. Within a week, the U.S.S.R. raised in the United Nations the question of the Peking Government's right to China's seat. This brought the disaccord

74

between Britain and the U.S.A. even more embarrassingly into the open; Britain's first reaction was to abstain from voting.[1]

It may be—though one certainly cannot be sure—that the U.S.A. might have come around to recognition of Communist China had no aggravating circumstance developed. But Senator McCarthy and the Korean War between them made any change in the American administration's position impossible and the issue remained an irritant that grew more aggravating with time.

However, none of this affected Britain's attitude to Mr. Truman's initial action over Korea in June, 1950, which Britain warmly applauded and, of course, actively supported. Indeed, though the British role in Korea was a modest one, it far exceeded that of any other American ally, save Turkey. By the end of 1950, the Turks excepted, the only foreign units fighting by the Americans' side in Korea were from the United Kingdom and the Commonwealth. From the first the war was seen in Britain as a necessary United Nations war, the product of deliberate aggression which, if unchecked, would infect any area in the world where Communism was pressing against the *status quo*. But it also became early apparent that the Korean conflict and the Chinese dispute were not going to remain uninfected each by the other. When on 27 June, 1950, Mr. Truman ordered the United States Seventh Fleet to neutralize Formosa it became apparent that, whatever the pros and cons of the action, it supplied a link between Chiang's struggle and Syngman Rhee's and meant an indefinite endorsement by the U.S.A. of the Formosa régime. Moreover, from the first moment, when General MacArthur was appointed as both the United States and the United Nations Commander-in-Chief in Korea, it could be foreseen that the waging of this United Nations war would create many problems.

However, as long as success attended allied arms, and the only enemy appeared to be the North Koreans, this hardly mattered. It was when the going got tougher and Chinese contingents began to appear, with all that they implied about extending the war, that the disagreements and prejudices over how to handle Mao and Chiang began to manifest themselves in this new context of an

[1] China's intervention in the Korean War brought a certain harmony into British and American attitudes in the United Nations; in June 1951 the United Kingdom supported a United States resolution to defer indefinitely the question of Chinese representation.

75

unequal Anglo-American partnership in arms. When, after the catastrophe on the Yalu River, Mr. Truman at a press conference on 30 November, 1950, appeared to be saying that the United States might order MacArthur to use the A-bomb at his discretion, a deep concern flared up not only in London but also in other West European capitals. MacArthur's discretion was not a quality the British found it easy to believe in. In the House of Commons a debate ensued which the American ambassador, Mr. Gifford, thought to be "the most serious, anxious and responsible debate on foreign affairs conducted . . . since the Labour Party came to power in 1945".[1] Mr. Attlee, after conferring with the French, flew immediately to Washington for a conference to which circumstances certainly lent an appearance of panic hardly appropriate for a concert of allies.

That Mr. Truman was in fact proposing to authorize the use of the bomb seems in retrospect unlikely. What comes out very clearly from the reports of the meeting which he and Mr. Attlee have provided[2] is that divergence of emphasis, more than plain contrariety of policy, marked the British and American positions. This was, of course, the consequence of those historical and geographical differences mentioned earlier. The great British anxieties reflected Britain's situation and connexions. The British anxiety was that large forces would get drawn into an Asiatic war and so leave Europe open to Russian invasions; this was a clear reflection of Britain's role as a European off-shore island. Her second was that either by use of the bomb or otherwise the war would develop exclusively the appearance of a war between "Europeans" and Asiatics; this undoubtedly reflected strong representations which Britain had received from the Asiatic members of the Commonwealth.

It was not to be expected that Mr. Attlee would secure from Mr. Truman any modification of the United States attitude towards the recognition of Peking and the seating of her representatives at the United Nations. What he did get was agreement on the importance of avoiding a general war in the East and on the continuing priority, in American planning, of Europe. His advocacy of negotiations in Korea, with its implication of a withdrawal to the 38th parallel, did

[1] Truman, op. cit., Vol. II (New York), p. 396; (London), p. 420.

[2] Ibid., Vol. II (New York), pp. 394–413; (London), pp. 418–38 and Francis Williams, op. cit., 236–240.

not win direct acceptance; it was an easier policy for a British Prime Minister to urge from Whitehall than for a Democratic United States President to impose on Congress, on MacArthur and—it may be added—on the North Koreans and their allies. Indeed there is no particular reason to suppose that MacArthur's dismissal four months later and the U.S.S.R.'s proposal of truce talks six weeks after that owed anything to British representations, acceptable as both events were in British eyes.

In retrospect it is not surprising that the later stages of the Korean War, so protracted, so indeterminate, should have imposed peculiar strains upon the alliance. No one had imagined that the war would prove so long and so costly. (Plenty of pessimists, of course, had predicted that it would develop into World War III; no one had anticipated that while still staying within its Korean confines it would prove such a running sore and nervous drain.) The longer the war continued the less clear became its objectives; the United Nations element seemed to recede and its place was largely taken by a vague concept of the war as an anti-Communist crusade. While some British opinion accepted this and almost all British opinion recognized that in some sense this was true, hardly anyone found this an adequate basis for continuing the war. For a policy of "containing" communism there was general support; for a "crusade" against it—especially one launched in the Far East—there was almost none. Indeed the American experience at this time with such self-appointed anti-Communist crusaders as Senator McCarthy was producing a tremendous backwash of suspicion and antipathy in Britain, heightened of course by the known "Asialationist" tendencies of such rabble-rousers.

The Korean conflict in fact brought out very clearly one of the problems which is attendant upon partnership in arms between two powers of unequal strength. In a sense (the sense which was almost always most vividly present to British minds) Britain had as much at stake in Korea as the U.S.A.: if anything went wrong with the calculations and a limited war was turned into a global one, Britain's chances of survival in any recognizable form were less even than those of the United States. Yet Britain's contribution to the common cause was almost negligible beside the Americans'. Exactly comparable figures are not easy to come by but the scale of the two war efforts is pretty well represented by the fact that in 1951 while the

U.S.A. had between 160,000 and 200,000 troops in Korea, the British had only 12,000.[1] As for casualties, the comparative figures, up to 19 August, 1953, the date of the armistice, were:

	U.S.A.	United Kingdom	Other Commonwealth
Dead	22,731	Dead or missing believed dead 958	Dead or missing believed dead 521
Wounded	105,961	2,556	1,190

(also United States missing 13,585, which helps to explain that by 1954 the total United States official figures of dead had risen to 33,629).

There were many good reasons why the British and the Commonwealth contribution should have been so modest; there were over 20,000 British troops actively engaged by themselves on a not wholly dissimilar war in Malaya and of course the whole Korean incident increased the tension in Europe and called for a general manning of the ramparts there. Nor indeed at any time did any responsible American soldier or official complain of Britain not pulling her weight. This, however, did not alter the fact that with so small a contribution Britain could not hope to have any real voice in any of the on-the-spot decisions. She had to accept a local leadership which was a hundred per cent American and rely on the slow, remote and inadequate processes of diplomatic representation to ensure that the local commanders would not authorize moves whose ultimate implications might be global.

From this point of view the United Nations auspices under which the war was formally fought were a doubtful blessing. Even if there had been no MacArthur there would have been a problem of co-ordination,[2] arising from a clash between the form and substance of the war. In form it was a United Nations war to which all members should have contributed and for which the United Nations should have been, if not the directing, at any rate the co-ordinating agency. In fact it was the Americans who supplied nine-tenths of

[1] Owing to the American practice of rotating tours of duty the Korean war made an even greater impact on American opinion at home than the numbers in Korea at any one time would suggest. The fact is the risk of Korea was real for every American household with a male of military age.

[2] As indeed there was when MacArthur had been succeeded by Ridgway.

the troops and did nine-tenths of the fighting (apart, of course, from the South Koreans themselves) and MacArthur as the U.S./ U.N. Supreme Commander reported to the United Nations only through the U.S. Joint Chiefs of Staff. Though weekly conferences were held by the U.N. "Committee of Sixteen", consisting of member governments who supplied forces for the Korean operation, all the military decisions were made outside the United Nations and in secret, as their nature dictated. The only formal framework for co-ordination was thus an unreal one, yet it served as an excuse to prevent anything more realistic being constructed. Most of the time there was only a very intermittent diplomatico-military liaison. The inadequacies of all Anglo-American military liaison in a Pacific setting were fortunately in part offset by the generally good relations which existed at the diplomatic level. Sir Anthony Eden recounts an example in his Memoirs, illustrating the ready responsiveness of Mr. Acheson :

"On one occasion I showed him a telegram from Mr. Selwyn Lloyd, the Minister of State, giving an account of feeling in the House of Commons with regard to Korea. After reading the telegram, Mr. Acheson said: 'In fact, you would like us to make fewer mistakes, and to keep you better informed when we do make them.' He went on to welcome the visit of Lord Alexander, then Minister of Defence, with Mr. Lloyd to Korea. 'I understand,' he said, 'the anxieties which the British public must be feeling, and I hope that this will do something to dispel them.'"[1]

Nothing could better oil the wheels of an alliance than this ready sympathy, and nothing could serve as a substitute were it lacking, yet the Anglo-American experience during the Korean War leaves one with a strong impression that such personal and *ad hoc* receptiveness was not enough. The advantages of the direct, informal approach, of working through a trusty friend at court, do not appear to have been a substitute for the kind of regular, committee type of consultation which predominated at all levels in World War II. The difficulties of establishing such a system in relation to Korea were obviously great; perhaps, having regard to the disparity of the forces involved and the peculiar personal and national tensions and strains attendant on the whole enterprise, they were

[1] Eden, op. cit., p. 21.

insuperable. The fact remains that their absence was not adequately made up in any other way.[1] Thus even as late as June, 1952, there could be a major flurry over the American action in bombing targets on the Yalu River, without informing Britain in advance, though there was an agreement to consult before any attack was made. The explanation was that what to the British appeared a development fraught with grave implications, to the Americans appeared a merely tactical measure, not covered by the agreement. The incident did indeed stimulate a new experiment in allied co-operation. On 28 July, 1952, the appointment was announced of Major-General S. N. Shoosmith of the British army to be Deputy Chief of Staff at General Clark's (the U.N./U.S. Commander-in-Chief's) Headquarters. His function was not to be a secret channel of information with London but, as a knowledgeable British representative, to be on the spot to advise General Clark about the probable British reactions to some proposed course of action.

However, there were disagreements between Britain and the U.S.A. on Far Eastern issues which persisted despite all consultation. In this category the long train of differences which flowed from the initial dispute over recognizing Red China was of conspicuous importance. The same concern for Hong Kong and trade which had been a factor in stimulating British recognition continued to operate throughout the Korean War to a degree which the Americans thought deplorable. (It was the old difference between a nation which must trade in order to live and one which lives in order, *inter alia*, to trade.) The total volume of British trade with China was small, but to Hong Kong it was vital; without it the colony could not survive and to forbid it might provoke China to move in and take over. Britain, like a good shopkeeper, was also concerned with keeping her connexion. Red China might be a poor customer, might even chivvy British firms and businessmen unmercifully; even so, it was better to hold on and maintain the connection than to let it go to competitors whom she would never

---

[1] Cf. Mr. Shinwell, former Minister of Defence, complaining reminiscently on 25 June, 1952, that the Labour government "were never satisfied with the consultation and co-operation that had been going on. We always pressed for more consultation but for some reason or other the United States administration resisted the pressure and we never received the satisfaction we desired." H.C. Deb., 5th Series, Vol. 502, col. 2356.

afterwards succeed in ousting. Consequently, though at the outbreak of the Korean War the Government prohibited the export of
many strategic materials to China, it was not prepared to go as far
as the U.S.A. and ban everything (just as the U.S.A. did not try to
ban all Japanese trade with the Chinese mainland). However, as
Chinese participation in the war became more blatant, American
pressure on Britain mounted and indeed even in Britain there was
a sense of shock when it was revealed that 77,624 tons of rubber
had gone from Malaya and Singapore to China in 1950 and that in
the first quarter of 1951 alone this had risen to 46,500 tons. In
May a strict limit of 2,500 tons a month was initially imposed and
later, in view of the stocks China might be supposed to have
accumulated, a total ban on rubber exports was imposed for the rest
of the war.

There was nothing here which had been kept secret from the
U.S.A. Indeed every fortnight the Hong Kong Government supplied the American authorities with a detailed list of commodities
exported to China.[1] But in the inflamed condition of American
opinion the superficial impression of Britain as a reluctant ally
trading with the enemy proved very nearly ineffaceable, and greatly
complicated the task of obtaining an American hearing for the
British case on the many Far Eastern issues over which there was
disagreement. It is doubtful whether the British case for continuing
trade with China ever got across to Americans. Paradoxically it was
harder to get a hearing for it after the cessation of general Korean
fighting than before. The new Republican administration seemed
alarmingly responsive to the pressures of McCarthyite congressional
opinion, which now was demanding a blockade of the China coast.
Such a blockade was doubly distasteful to Britain; not only would
it affect trade; worse still, it would provoke incidents which might
easily result in open conflict with China. To avert such a development and appease the American demand, the United Kingdom
introduced in March, 1953, a strict licensing system for vessels
journeying to Chinese ports. As appeasement this hardly worked;
within a few months it was followed by a set of restrictive moves
by the United States Government against foreign shipping designed
apparently to make any trading with China unprofitable, however

[1] This was the list from which General MacArthur read out to the
Senate Committee the alarming catalogue of critical items, omitting
only to indicate that in each case the quantities supplied were *nil*.

non-strategic the materials. Even after the armistice was signed on 27 June, 1953, there was little improvement. Sir Winston Churchill told Parliament on 17 December that trade with China was among the topics he discussed with the President in their meeting at Bermuda but evidently no progress was made. In the absence of a peace settlement the United Nations embargo on strategic exports remained in force, and the 480 items which the United Kingdom bound itself not to export to China were almost twice as many as those on the embargo list for the U.S.S.R. and its satellites in Europe.

Meanwhile in Japan Britain and the U.S.A. worked on a rather different problem, the making of a peace treaty, and the status and powers which an ex-enemy country should enjoy under it. The U.S.A., mentor of a "westernized" Japan, felt a certain pride of sponsorship in presenting this Far Eastern Eliza Doolittle for admission to democratic society. No such sentiments sweetened the natural sourness of Australian and New Zealand feelings towards a former bitter combatant and Britain, though somewhat less antipathetic herself, had to take note of the sentiments of those Commonwealth members whom she had not been able to protect in 1942 and who had lived so much closer to the Japanese menace than she had herself. For her own part, her major concern, once again, was with trade; what were the implications for British industry of a sovereign Japan, able to indulge in unregulated, undercutting competition?

The Truman administration had entrusted the negotiations over the treaty to that eminent representative of the opposition party, John Foster Dulles. Mr. Dulles pursued his consultations not only with the relevant allied embassies in Washington but also in a series of visits to allied capitals. But consultation itself raised a familiar problem. What about China? Mr. Dulles sent a copy of the draft treaty to the tenants of Formosa; the British Government proposed that it should be submitted to the Communist Government in Peking. Once Britain had recognized Peking this was a logical enough corollary to the argument that all the anti-Japanese allies of World War II should be consulted. Britain was supported in her position by India and the other states which had also granted recognition—including, of course, the U.S.S.R. Nothing, however, could better illustrate the sterile controversy into which the recognition dispute plunged the allies, since it was perfectly evident that on this issue nothing but obstruction could possibly come from Peking. Moreover, there was, of course, a good deal more at stake than "mere" recognition. Amongst the rights which Japan was renouncing under the treaty were her claims to Formosa and the Pescadores. Who was she renouncing them to? To Chiang Kai-shek or to Mao Tse-tung? The Americans, as might be expected, were adamant in their refusal to let the Peking Government have anything to do with the treaty and for two months a brisk controversy ran its course. At first the British seem seriously to have considered delaying the treaty until the question of the two Chinas should have been settled, but sensibly they concluded that delay would be a worse alternative. But the near deadlock which had developed on the China question could only be resolved by a negative compromise; it was agreed that neither of the Chinas should be invited to the Peace Conference or asked to comment upon the treaty. The result cost both Britain and the U.S.A. some support from their friends; the Indians and Burmese, supporters of Peking, declined to be parties to the treaty; the Formosan Government presented an indignant protest and the Generalissimo complained to Mr. Dewey of the U.S.A.'s "total abandonment" of her wartime ally.

The consequential bad blood did not end there. The compromise which Mr. Herbert Morrison, as British Foreign Secretary, had arranged with Mr. Dulles meant, of course, that it would be left to Japan herself to decide, after the treaty was signed, what relations with which China she would adopt. In line with this, at the San Francisco Peace Conference in September, at which the treaty was signed, Mr. Dulles explicitly ruled out the exertion of "a compulsion in this matter which would create resentment in Japan and . . . activate and aggravate Allied division". For Britain more was at stake than the mere desire to get backing for her recognition policy. There was also an important commercial interest involved. In one region of Britain the Japanese Treaty had been received with nothing but dislike and apprehension. Lancashire saw the full resumption by Japan of her sovereignty as a sign that her old competitor in the cotton markets of the world would start price-cutting, copyright infringement, false labelling and "unfair" labour practices again. But since no effective controls could possibly be written into the treaty it became all important whether Japan would again find an outlet, as before the war, in the mainland of China or whether, excluded from there, she would be fighting Britain for markets throughout the rest of the East. Obviously her decision about which government to recognize would have a crucial bearing on this.

It is not enough, however, for treaties to be drafted and signed; they have also to be ratified. Under the American constitution this can become a convenient opportunity for the Senate to introduce modifications, express or implied, to the agreements which her own and other executives have approved. That something of this kind might occur over the Japanese treaty was already being rumoured by the autumn of 1951, provoking from Mr. Kenneth Younger who, as Labour Minister of State, had been associated with the treaty-making, a reminder and a warning:

> "I sincerely trust that no such situation will arise. I am quite sure that it would not be the wish of any of those engaged on behalf of the United States in negotiating this Treaty, and I know it would be regarded, not only by them, but certainly by the representatives of many of the nations who signed the Treaty, as a clear departure from the understanding upon which this question was left on one side by the signatories at San Francisco."[1]

To supplement this, in Mr. Eden's words, we made "our views absolutely plain to the United States Government on a considerable number of occasions".[2] Nonetheless, in December, 1951, while ratification was still pending in the U.S.A. Mr. Dulles and two members of the Senate Committee on Foreign Relations visited Tokio and there did their "best to make known to the Japanese Government and the Japanese people" "the wish of the United States Government"[3] that Japan should recognize the Formosa Government. As a result Mr. Yoshida, the Prime Minister, gave an undertaking that his Government would as soon as possible conclude a treaty which would recognize the Nationalist régime in Formosa as the government of China. There was a splutter of impotent indignation in Britain over what was universally regarded as a piece of sharp practice and Mr. Eden's sour comment to the

[1] HC Deb., 5th series, Vol. 494, col. 895–6, 26 November, 1951.

[2] Ibid., Vol. 495, col. 166, 30 January, 1952.

[3] Statement by Senator Sparkman, *Congressional Record*, 16 January, 1952. (Vol. 98, p. 219)

House of Commons on the episode was that "fortunately there are not many such topics between us and the United States Government".[1]

Another by-product of the Japanese Treaty was the A.N.Z.U.S. Pact which had important consequences for the balance of power, as between Britain and the United States, in the Pacific. If Japan was to be restored to her sovereign status, she must be given the right to re-arm. How then were Australia and New Zealand to be protected against the menace of a revival of aggressive Japanese militarism? Their lively fears on this score were pressed throughout all the treaty negotiations and at the request of Australia and New Zealand the U.S.A. simultaneously explored arrangements for a Pacific security pact. By April, 1951, matters were far enough advanced for Mr. Truman to announce broad lines of agreement and on 1 September a three-power treaty was signed at San Francisco.

In British eyes the A.N.Z.U.S. pact, as it became known, was open to two objections. It isolated the defence of the South-West Pacific from the defence needs of the whole area, particularly Malaya and Singapore, and it pointedly excluded Britain from membership. Though kept informed by Australia and New Zealand throughout the negotiations, Britain had not been invited to participate in them. For the first time in history member states of the Commonwealth[2] had entered into defence arrangements with another power from which the mother country was excluded; this, despite the fact that Britain's Commonwealth commitments would of course immediately involve her on their side if they were attacked. The fact that their chosen protector was the U.S.A. reduced, but by no means obliterated, the mortification involved. The Conservative opposition attacked the Labour Government for not having represented Britain's claims to A.N.Z.U.S. membership strongly enough, but when his turn came to assume the reins of government Mr. Churchill could not do any better than his predecessor. When the Pacific Council set up by the A.N.Z.U.S. Pact was due to hold its first meeting in Hawaii in August, 1952, Britain made a request to be allowed to send an observer; even this was refused at the insistence, it was generally believed, of the

[1] HC Deb., 5th series, Vol. 495, col. 166.

[2] Apart from Canada, whose contiguity to the United States was always judged to put her in a special position.

United States. The reason given was that to admit Britain would entail admitting France, the Philippines and other powers with Pacific interests, even perhaps Japan. In British ears this hardly sounded convincing, in view of Britain's special relations with Australia and New Zealand and the fact that she maintained a navy in the area and controlled its western approaches through her base at Singapore. In American eyes, however, this last argument worked the other way round since they were anxious not to have to extend the pact to involve any commitment to the defence of Singapore, much less Malaya.

All this might or might not be true. What was painfully certain was that it reflected a decline in United Kingdom potency in the Pacific area. Indeed it was precisely this decline which was the basic reason for A.N.Z.U.S. coming into being at all. Nor was it an entirely new phenomenon. It went back to the situation in the late 30's when the United Kingdom had, in effect, abdicated as a Pacific policeman in favour of the U.S.A., reluctant as America was to assume that role. War intensified this. When France fell, Britain had to warn Australia and New Zealand that if Japan came into the war no British fleet could be sent to the Far East and they would have to rely on the United States. When Japan did come in, this was what did happen, and the fact that Singapore was British did not prevent its collapse. It was the United States which filled the defence vacuum and the move of General MacArthur from the Philippines to Australia in 1942 was symbolic. The presence of American sailors, soldiers and marines in Australia literally brought home the fact of American preponderance. The return of peace did not change any of these power relationships; it merely glossed them over for a while until the restoration of Japanese sovereignty forced them to the surface once again. In a sense it was only another logical consequence of the growing-up of the Commonwealth, the attainment by Australia and New Zealand of that direct relationship with the U.S.A. which Canada had so long enjoyed. In that sense it was true, as Mr. Menzies said, that the treaty was "only a local manifestation of closer British-American relations".[1] But the firm exclusion of Britain from that relationship had no real parallel in the Canadian case; it was in no sense contributory to the purposes of the pact; it was, in fact, an institutionalized expression in peace of the Pacific exclusiveness which the U.S.A. had practised in war.

[1] *Annual Register*, 1952, p. 81.

The disagreements between Britain and the U.S.A. over Far
Eastern questions did not much diminish as the fifties wore on.
There was, however, a slow but noticeable diminution in the heat
of their altercations. There were good reasons for this. McCarthyism
and its ally, the China Lobby, lost ground in the United States.
Opinion there, at all levels, learnt a new patience from the final
frustrations of the Korean War. Awareness spread of the imperfec-
tions of America's staunchest, but also most embarrassing, allies,
Chiang Kai-shek and Syngman Rhee. Japan's gradual rediscovery
of her own personality brought with it (as in the anti-American
demonstrations which led President Eisenhower to cancel his Tokio
visit in 1960) some sobering re-assessments of America's mission in
the Far East. On the British side the obstinate refusal of the Communist Government of China to respond with civility to British
recognition, the irrefutable demonstrations of its aggressiveness,
towards Tibet and towards India—quite apart from Korea and
Laos—left fewer illusions about the amenability of Peking to fair
words and soft treatment.

When President Eisenhower took over from Mr. Truman the
initial disposition in Britain was to fear that a new "forward"
policy would be launched against the Chinese Communists, in
response to all the "China Lobby" elements in the Republican
Party. The decision in February, 1953, to use the Seventh Fleet as
a "one-way shield" (i.e. to revoke its orders to restrain a Nationalist
attack on the Communist mainland) lent colour to this view and
excited proportionate alarm in Britain. This was indeed a trying
time for the alliance in the Far East, when an inherently tricky
situation seemed often to be aggravated by the sabre-rattling of
American military spokesmen and the application of the principles
of "brinkmanship" by Mr. John Foster Dulles. A fuller treatment
of that technique is reserved for the following chapter, but whatever may be thought about its employment in general and the
strains it imposed upon America's European allies in particular,
one result certainly was to impose a kind of *Pax Americana* upon
the Far East during President Eisenhower's first term and for a
while after. There was no war; Communist Chinese aggression
against Korea, Japan, Formosa and other island areas was, if
seriously intended, not carried out.

The price, in terms of British nerves, was at times certainly high.
When after the first shelling of Quemoy and Matsu the United

States in 1954 negotiated the mutual defence treaty with Formosa it seemed a risky hostage that she was giving to fortune. And even though it was followed by a Nationalist undertaking not to attack the mainland without American approval, the President at the same time secured from Congress authority to protect not only Formosa but also the "related positions"—i.e. if he chose so to regard them, the off-shore islands. The elements of ambiguity which Mr. Dulles claimed to constitute the strength of this policy were, in British eyes, its most serious weakness. Yet, looking back, one has to admit that in some sense, as a temporary measure, it worked. Tension fell; in April, 1955, Chou En-lai proposed bilateral talks. A certain *détente* ensued; begun at Geneva in August, the talks dragged on inconclusively until 1958. The trouble was that they settled nothing and "tension", with its concomitant of Chinese shelling of the islands, began again, to persist intermittently down to the present day. The prospect is not a reassuring one. As China's strength grows, and the Seventh Fleet remains in situ and American commitments to Formosa are unchanged, the inherent dangers of the situation are likely to increase.

Directly, of course, none of this has involved Britain as an active partner to the United States. Her interest has been more negative than positive—to prevent the outbreak of a war which would do her no good and might easily prove catastrophic. Consequently her most overt concern has always been to reduce tension in the area and diminish the risk of an unplanned explosion. Yet it would be less than honest to ignore a subordinate but very tangible interest which she has always had in the preservation of Formosan independence. Hong Kong too is an off-shore island. It has existed under British rule, on Chinese sufferance, because no doubt it has been to mutual advantage that such a status should continue. Yet how long, one must ask, if American power were withdrawn and if Formosa fell into Communist hands, would Hong Kong remain a British possession and a bastion of capitalist enterprise upon Communist shores? To that extent whether she likes it or not Britain too has her investment in the Far East *status quo*.

To say Hong Kong is, of course, to say "trade with China" and on this issue the divergent points of view described earlier also persisted throughout the fifties. At length indeed, in the calmer conditions of President Eisenhower's second term and the Macmillan-Eisenhower post-Suez rapprochement, some agreement was contrived. But it was an agreement to differ. The long-pressed British claim that China should be put on all fours with the U.S.S.R. in respect of the goods which she could buy from the West still made no converts in Washington. But at least it proved possible in June, 1957, to obtain indulgence for a British decision to abolish the "Chinese differential" and adopt the same embargo list for China and the U.S.S.R. The results were not, in fact, striking but they were a step towards normalization of relations between China and the West.[1]

Normalization indeed remained the goal of British policy, however hard it might be to attain. For the U.S.A., as long as the Republicans remained in power, even Eisenhower Republicans, it was unthinkable. But time, the United Nations and the pragmatism of Mr. Kennedy might, if combined, effect some gradual change. The steady erosion of support for America's policy of preventing Peking from occupying the Chinese seat at the U.N. led in 1961 to some fresh thinking in Washington. Britain, after a long period of abstention, now went on record as publicly affirming her long-held conviction that the government she recognized in China should be the government she would recognize in the U.N. The United States Government did not change its public professions, nor yet its private preferences, but in conceding, however reluctantly, that the General Assembly might consider the question of Chinese representation it was beginning the painful process of realigning desire and reality.

---

[1] Cf. Mr. Maudling speaking to the press in Washington on 14 June, 1960, as reported by Reuter: "Britain's trade with Communist China was small but useful, and was limited by China's inability to pay. Britain believed in maintaining restrictions on exports of strategic goods, but on the whole the flow of trade between countries tends to break down barriers and to make it a little easier to achieve successful human relations."

7

SOUTH-EAST ASIA

IN South-East Asia many of the factors which operated in Far East politics turned up again, to determine, and often to complicate, relations between Britain and the United States. Priorities, however, were somewhat different. Here was a region largely permeated, historically, by British rule, influence or trade. It bordered, for the most part, on waters such as the Indian Ocean and the Straits of Sumatra still dominated, strategically, by the British navy. These same waters (and the air above them) still constituted a vital communications area for the Commonwealth, both for the immediately contiguous members such as Pakistan, India, Ceylon and Malaya and for the more remote territories of Australasia. For the U.S.A. these same factors of history and geography worked to remove the area from the centre of American interest. It owed little to American enterprise, had meant little for American strategy,[1] and exercised little or no sway over American sentiment.

But one complicating factor was common to both South-East Asia and to the Far East, the pressing threat of Communism, incorporated largely in the mass of mainland China, whose great bulk bordered the whole area on its eastern and northern flanks and whose agents infiltrated it at a thousand points. In the military resistance to this pressure Britain and France, in Malaya and in Indo-China, filled much the same role as the U.S.A. filled in North Korea, though with subtly different attitudes and expectations. In the ideological defence, the main British reliance was on the Commonwealth tie and the blend of local nationalisms and western democracy and administration. Economically, the area looked for aid first to the Commonwealth but also, since that of itself did not begin to be adequate, to the U.S.A. as well.

Save in Malaya, the general philosophy animating British atti-

[1] At least until the "domino" theory was elaborated in Eisenhower's first presidency by which Indo-China was likened to the first of a row of standing dominoes whose fall would bring down in succession Burma, Thailand, Malaya, Indonesia, the Philippines, Formosa and Japan.

tudes to Communism in the area was one of containment. If the Malayan struggle against the guerrillas had about it an element of the crusade, this was partly because Communism here directly menaced a major British economic (and quasi-strategic) interest, the rubber crop and the tin mines, but just as much because it could fairly easily be identified with alien exploitation of the territory and turned back by an intensive effort which relied on local support. Here an all-out drive against the Communist guerillas bore little or no aspect of "West" against "East" or "colonialists" against native "liberators"; moreover, it could be fully self-contained, carrying virtually no risk of involvement with the great reservoir of Communist power, China herself. In Malaya it was the Communists who were over-extended, not their extirpators. Elsewhere, however, different conditions prevailed. No such secure base, either in geography or in local psychology or economics, existed for a comparable drive by the French in Indo-China; here the dice were loaded against a colonial occupying power, even in the phase of abdication and transfer of authority. The drain which the unequal struggle imposed on France was formidable. The Indo-China war not only prevented her making her proporationate contribution to N.A.T.O.; it ate at the vitals of the Fourth Republic itself, enfeebling its will and bringing the institutions into contempt.

In retrospect it seems fairly obvious that there was a basic identity of British and American objectives in this area; both powers wanted to contain Communism without extending the conflict to a point which involved an open war with China. However in the attempt to evolve a joint diplomacy which would realize these objectives they were doubtfully successful. This was partly their own fault, partly that of the French, who were divided in their purposes and leadership, wishing at one time for a massive Anglo-American military intervention and at another for a negotiated settlement which would enable them to contract out of the whole impossible business. This division in French attitudes corresponded in a considerable degree to the schizophrenia which the Chinese issue had created in American opinion, between the desire to settle scores with the Communists once and for all and the wish to end the Korean war and bring the boys back home. Splits in a national psyche, when they are as profound as this, almost always reveal themselves in the make-up of the individual national leaders as well; they were certainly reflected in 1950–4 in the public pronouncements of American leaders on the Indo-China problem (as on the Korean issue). At the same time it now seems reasonably certain that neither Mr. Eisenhower nor even Mr. Dulles (nor their predecessors, Mr. Truman and Mr. Acheson) had any intention of taking any action in Indo-China such as would involve the U.S.A. in an open war with China. Since this was at all times the aim of British diplomacy how did it come about that we so often and so painfully appeared to be at cross purposes in this part of the world? The answers to this question have an importance which transcends the local and historical situation in Indo-China in the early 1950's.

Some of the tactical divergencies between London and Washington could be explained by the different assessments of the local situation reaching the policy-makers from the men on the spot. In areas as confused as Indo-China it was easy for discrepant rumours and rationalizations to arise, and hard to ground any intelligence report in an unassailable basis of fact. From a welter of conflicting estimates each side could and almost inevitably did select those which best corresponded to its own preferred course of action. Even when, as often happened, the British and the Americans pooled their intelligence, this consequence was not averted.

The prepared policies then owed more, in the last resort, to the officials at home than to the men on the spot. As such they reflected, inevitably, the whole complex of national interests and attitudes towards the area such as were touched on at the opening of this chapter. The paradox was that seemingly Britain, with more at stake in South-East Asia than the U.S.A., was yet the more reluctant to countenance any deeper local involvement. When on 29 December, 1953, Mr. Dulles announced that in the event of an invasion of Indo-China, the American reaction "would not necessarily be confined to the particular theatre chosen by the Communists for their operations" and when on 12 January, 1954, he warned that Chinese intervention would have "grave consequences which might not be confined to Indo-China", both pronouncements aroused grave concern in the United Kingdom—far graver than in the U.S.A. When they were followed up in April, 1954, by American proposals of a joint allied warning to the Chinese against continued interference in Indo-China, the British contention was that the threat would be ineffective by itself, and if made real by military action would involve the allies in an outright Chinese war. When

Mr. Dulles and Admiral Radford urged Anglo-American intervention to save Dien-Bien-Phu, or to rally morale after its collapse,
Sir Winston Churchill's comment, according to Sir Anthony Eden,
was that "what we were being asked to do was to assist in misleading Congress into approving a military operation, which would in
itself be ineffective, and might well bring the world to the verge
of a major war".[1] On the basis of this reasoning the United Kingdom declined any participation in such a venture.

Behind this disharmony lay a good deal of sheer diplomatic
ineptness, intensified by the tendency of the American Government
to speak with more than one voice. But when all this has been
ironed away there remain, as can now be clearly seen, certain basic
reasons for the failure of the two allies to evolve an agreed Indo-
China policy in 1954. Since the Americans were making most of
the running, these reasons can best be observed initially in a study
of their proposed policies.

The technique of "brinkmanship" which they embodied and
which came to be associated with the diplomacy of Mr. Dulles was
in essence no more than an attempt to use against the Communists
the technique which the Communists often used against the West,
namely to threaten vague but ominous armed retaliation in an endeavour to deter or dissuade the other side from some contemplated
course of action. It is a technique as old as diplomacy itself but the
diplomat who would employ it successfully must be able to rely
upon unanimity within the government for which he speaks, perfect
liaison with his allies and complete mutual trust between himself
and his allied colleagues. Unfortunately the government in which
Mr. Dulles served was habitually given to thinking its diverse
thoughts aloud in public, the machinery of liaison between it and
its allies was intermittent and unreliable in its day-to-day workings,
and Mr. Dulles himself had not established a relationship of mutual
confidence with his fellow Foreign Secretaries in the allied camp.
Moreover, as the spokesman for a democracy which had foresworn
the employment of war as an instrument of national policy, Mr.
Dulles was at a continuous disadvantage in using the "brinkmanship" ploy in a manner which would be both convincing to the
enemy and acceptable to his publics at home and abroad. If, with
all these drawbacks, this device continued to be a feature of his
diplomacy, particularly *vis-à-vis* Communist China, the reasons

[1] Eden, op. cit., p. 105.

must be sought in a set of considerations which were peculiarly American.

The American administration was under continuous and heavy pressure at home from Congressmen, Senators and others whose epousal of a crusading policy in Asia was unrestrained by any consideration for America's obligations in Europe or any realistic appraisal of the prospects of military success in Asia. They were the one-idea men of the "China Lobby", whose advice the President hardly ever took, but whose importance in the Republican Party obliged him to make gestures and pronouncements which were often embarrassing for American policy and to outsiders often appeared truly alarming. The "China Lobby's" advocacy of forthright military action did, moreover, evoke a good deal of popular support because it rested on the inviting assumption that no large, Korean-like operation by ground troops would be needed to effect it. Their talk was always of an air strike or of naval action, reviving memories of the easy successes of the air raids on Japan or the memorable triumphs of the Leyte Gulf in the late war. "The bomb" would once again do it all; it was the "Maxim gun" mentality over again. The easy, even, as it seemed, hubristic self-confidence of the air and naval spokesman of this school reflected the *esprit de corps* of the two most pampered elements in the American armed services, the Strategic Air Command and the Pacific Fleet. In Washington they constituted powerful lobbies in their own right; Congressmen vied with each other to anticipate their demands for funds. Finally, behind the "China Lobby" and the pressures of certain strategists, was a pervasive public mood particularly receptive to simple solutions of Asiatic problems, a mood powerfully affected by the unaccustomed, frustrating, even humiliating "non-success" of the Korean enterprise. Although basically pacific, Americans in such a mood were indulgent to any advocates of a short way with Asiatic Communism, and very suspicious of any diplomatic or other dealings with the mammon of unrighteousness. Negotiation and neutralism were thus equally heretical; in particular if advocated by European spokesmen, they were likely to be regarded as signs of the guilty conscience of colonialism seeking to appease the Lucifer of Communism.

Not only were almost all these attitudes alien to the viewpoint of British administration, of whatever party complexion. They had not even any counterpart in any substantial section of British public opinion. In Britain there was no China Lobby, there was no Korea or post-Korea mood. The Malaya operation was as protracted as Korea and, to its participants, no less wearing. But it was, by comparison a clear success and, in any case, its reverberations on the home front were faint and few compared with those of Korea on the U.S.A.; few British soldiers were involved and, to a nation long accustomed to having some part of its forces soldiering *in partibus infidelium*, the operation had nothing especially abnormal about it.

But if the United Kingdom minded less about what Asian fighting there was, it minded a good deal more about what fighting there might be—or perhaps one should more strictly say, was more vividly aware of the dangers inherent in any extension of the fighting. No one can know for certain how much Mr. Dulles's "brinkmanship" frightened the enemy, but it was very apparent how much it frightened us. This is a likely risk in any alliance in any part of the world—that what seems a safe hazard to the leader whose finger is on the trigger will seem a mad gamble to those who line up behind him. But in South-East Asia, as in Korea, the United Kingdom had special reasons for deploring and resisting "brinkmanship". It feared a war in Asia not merely for what it would be in itself, but for the diversion it would be bound to cause in Europe; all the familiar "Atlantic First" arguments were just as operative in the 1950's as in the 1940's. It had also what probably was a truer assessment of the psychological hazards of "brandishing the bomb" in Asia. Though not lacking a certain vein of self-righteousness, the arguments put forward by British spokesmen on this issue were probably valid—that since the atom bomb had so far been used exclusively by the "whites" against the "yellows" Asiatics regarded it as more than just a super-weapon; to them it appeared as an instrument of genocide, the super-symbol of race war. To the extent to which this was so, even threats of the bomb's employment, it could be argued, harmed the cause of the West amongst the "uncommitted" elements in Asia. This did not mean that the British favoured any kind of nuclear disarmament in the East. We have Eden's word for it that British diplomacy relied hardly less than the Americans on "the deterrent power of the hydrogen bomb. I was grateful for it. I do not believe that we should have got through the Geneva Conference and avoided a major war without it".[1] The disagreement was largely over diplomatic technique. How did you use the deterrent? By brandishing it publicly? Or by invoking it discreetly? It corresponded, almost, to the difference between old world diplomacy and new.

Time and time again it was a solicitude for the "uncommitted" elements that characterized British as opposed to United States policy in South-East Asia. To leaders such as Dulles the condition of being "uncommitted" was itself deplorable; by British policy throughout all the post-war period it was generally accepted as a tolerable substitute for positive alignment with the West. Sometimes this was because Britain took an unduly rosy view of Asiatic Communism, as in the early days of Mao Tse-tung, but also it was a by-product of the British relationship with India. Indeed it is not too much to say that Britain's whole view of Asia was coloured by her Indian experiences. The one great post-war venture which had turned out better than was feared was the granting of independence to the Indian sub-continent; the great pleasant surprise of a decade which was generally marked by a decline of British power and influence was the decision of India and Pakistan to remain within the Commonwealth. And this not only established a gratifying relationship; it also created a new set of obligations and attitudes. For the first time the Commonwealth family became multi-racial, with the Asiatic voice entitled to a large share in its councils. And when the spokesman for that voice was the persuasive Mr. Nehru it was seldom that Whitehall failed to listen. Whitehall did not always agree with what he said, but it always took him seriously and always insisted, when dealing with Washington, that he was important not only in his own right as spokesman for India but also as a representative voice, sometimes even the representative voice of Asia.

The Americans were by no means always ready to accept this. In accordance with that basic moral law of Anglo-American relations by which we each deplore the other's transgressions and champion the cause of each other's underdogs, American opinion had been very pro-Indian during the long years of waning British rule. Mr. Roosevelt himself had not been above offering Mr. Churchill recurrent advice on the subject. But India independent seemed to lose for Americans much of the charm of India struggling to be free and Mr. Nehru seemed a poor reincarnation of

[1] Eden, op. cit., p. 123.

Mahatma Gandhi. It was partly that the war promoted General and Mrs. Chiang Kai-shek into a first place in America's Asiatic affections from which no rival could hope to dislodge them, but it was also a result of the policies which the newly independent India chose to pursue—something very like socialism at home and neutralism abroad. The first was venial, the second much less so, particularly when it involved not only the recognition of Communist China but also a good deal of (as it turned out) optimistic assessments of the new China's course and attitudes. Incarnated in Mr. Krishna Menon's performances at the United Nations, the Indian disposition to lecture both sides impartially, or worse still, as it often seemed, partially, grated sharply on the American consciousness. By contrast, Americans found Pakistan sympathetic and responsive. The Moslem mood was closer to North American activism than the Hindu—at least where anti-Communism was the issue. And there was no Pakistani Menon to behave like a moralizing Mephistopheles in New York.

In Whitehall, the Foreign Office constantly endeavoured to associate India whenever possible with any diplomatic negotiations or arrangements involving the Far East or South-East Asia, even at the risk of provoking from Mr. Dulles his oft-quoted complaint that British policy was subject to a veto from Delhi. Apart from their solicitude for the Commonwealth connexion, the British defended this deference to the Indian viewpoint on the dual grounds that India constituted a certain link, or channel of communication with Peking and that she had an interest of her own in securing the stability of the area. The first argument cut both ways in Washington; it would only work where some agreement or *modus vivendi* with Peking was accepted as desirable, as in the negotiation of a Korean armistice, though even so the Indian role as mediator was liable to prove, in American eyes, a suspect one, as in the disputes over the repatriation of prisoners. The second argument hardly admitted of rebuttal, but was liable to evoke a corollary not very acceptable to Britain—that if the United Kingdom put forward India, the U.S.A. would advance the claims of Chiang Kai-shek. This was the American contention even in a context as unsuitable as the formation of the South-East Treaty Organization. Mr. Dulles, according to Sir Anthony Eden, "explained that if there was any question of extending the security arrangements westwards to include India, there would be a 'strong demand' in the

United States to extend it eastwards as well, to include Nationalist China and Japan . . . I did not like (said Sir Anthony) this balancing of India against Formosa. The two did not seem to me comparable."[1] The State Department however persisted in the attitude assumed by its chief and "repeated its warning that any attempt to include India would be countered by the inclusion of Formosa".[2]

Whether indeed any more accommodating American attitude would have affected Indian policy on this particular issue remains doubtful. India in 1954 was too deeply committed to a thoroughgoing neutralism: even the Chinese takeover of Tibet had not yet affected India's public stand. Paradoxically indeed, any overt shift in India's position would probably have destroyed her value to the democracies no less than to the Communists as a viable and reliable neutral, whose services at Panmunjon and later as Chairman of the three-power supervisory commission for the Indo-China settlement were almost indispensable. In that sense, though she was not a member of the Geneva Conference, India's support for its solutions was a pre-condition of its success.

Ironically, almost the same could be said of the U.S.A. The American dislike of the whole Geneva operation was intense, involving as it did sitting down at the same table with the Chinese Communists and bargaining about the precise extent to which they should be allowed to retain gains which they had no right to in the first place. Moreover the Americans could claim with some justice that they had been put into this position as a result of the failure of one of their major allies, the French, to make their colonialist régime in Indo-China acceptable or to construct a viable local administration on their colonialist foundations. Thus grumbles about "colonialism" were uttered in the same breath as dire threats about air strikes in defence of Dien Bien Phu, and Mr. Dulles absented himself from almost the whole of the Geneva proceedings even though the U.S.A. was a major participant in the conference. Indeed there was the supreme and especially painful irony that in a real sense the success of the conference was due to the U.S.A.; Eden's patient diplomacy may have been the efficient cause of the agreements on the cease-fire and the partition of Vietnam, but it was the knowledge of American atomic might which made the Communist powers want an agreement at all. Yet, since the agree-

[1] Eden, op. cit., p. 97.
[2] Ibid., p. 98.

ments presented concessions to the enemy, not only of territory but also of human beings (the armistice line legalized the passing under the Viet Minh of over twelve million people), they were too distasteful to be openly endorsed by the American Government. Mr. Dulles told Mr. Eden that it would be difficult to "persuade Congress to guarantee, in effect, the Communist domination of North Vietnam" and so the U.S.A. did not in fact associate them-selves with the final declaration of the conference. Instead in a unilateral statement the United States Government announced that it would refrain from disturbing the cease-fire agreements by force or by the threat of force and would view any forcible violation of them with grave concern. It is hardly profitable to inquire how far this was a moral concession by Mr. Dulles's right hand to his left, and how far it was a political concession by the American executive to the American legislature and to the intransigent elements in the Republican Party.[1] For our purpose it is more important to note the severe strain which the unequal sharing of the Geneva burden placed on Anglo-American relations and particularly on the per-sonal relations of Mr. Dulles and Mr. Eden, each regarding the other as making up his own rules for playing what was supposed to be a common game.

Thus the Geneva Conference displayed with painful clarity the difficulties of the alliance in executing a tactical retreat from an untenable position. And after the retreat there was still the re-grouping. To get a settlement and to make the settlement stick, it was almost certainly necessary at the same time to be affirming a collective will to stand firm on the positions newly taken up. But however necessary, it was a ticklish operation to combine the pacific motions of the conference table with the belligerent gestures associated with building up an alliance. Here too the Eden-Dulles partnership proved barely equal to the strain which tactical neces-sity imposed upon it. In Europe, thanks mainly to the clear and firm boundary line between east and west and the overwhelming and unmistakable effectiveness of American atomic power, there had been the time and assurance necessary to build the N.A.T.O.

[1] Mr. Dulles might perhaps have claimed that this sort of "moral" stand over the whole Geneva operation was an indispensable pre-condition of his securing from Congress the large slice of economic aid for India for which he successfully pleaded while the Geneva agree-ments were being concluded.

structure with adequate deliberation, stage by stage. Moreover, although American support had been absolutely crucial, the organization had sprung from local initiative and rested on a firm local will to resist. In South-East Asia, on the other hand, the boundary line between Communists and anti-Communists was neither clear nor firm and although American atomic power was an ever-present asset the whole allied experience in Korea had shown that it was in no sense a substitute for conventional forces on the ground and that too crude an exploitation of the psychology of the deterrent could easily boomerang. The greatest obstacle, however, to the speedy construction of an anti-Communist "shield" was the weakness of the South-East Asian polities themselves; local initiative hardly existed; local wills to resist had to be carefully fostered and sustained; there was only the most embryonic common regional feeling. From this it was possible to draw either of two opposite conclusions. To the Americans, shocked by the Vietnam collapse, these local weaknesses only made the more urgent the throwing up of some system of collective defence, however imperfect. If Indo-China was the first domino even its partial fall made remedial action imperative. To the British, however, the argument worked the other way; not only were they anxious to get the Geneva Conference over first, but in addition they were very conscious of the need for conciliatory diplomatic groundwork designed to secure the participation, if possible, of India and her neighbours or, if active participation could not be secured, at any rate their passive benevolence. We wanted a pact, not only because we wished to secure an American commitment to the safeguarding of such possessions as Malaya and Hong Kong, but also because we hoped to repair thereby some of the damage done to our Pacific position by our exclusion from A.N.Z.U.S.[1] This made it difficult for us to insist as much as we should have wished on comprehensive advance preparation. Nevertheless the United Kingdom did secure a very reluctant United States agreement to approaching the five Colombo powers, India, Pakistan, Ceylon, Burma and Indonesia while the pact was still in the planning stage. It was no use. With varying degrees of coolness all except Pakistan announced their non-partici-

[1] Meeting in Washington on 30 June, 1954, the representatives of the A.N.Z.U.S. powers had announced their "vital concern" with the S.E. Asia area and their agreement on the need for "immediate action" on setting up collective defence there.

pation. Plainly, had they come in, it could only have been into a broader, less pugnacious type of organization that would not be focused on the menace of Chinese aggression which obsessed the United States.

Consequently when the organizing conference met in September, 1954, it was at Manila, capital of a country which only a year before had negotiated a mutual defence treaty with the United States, and of the eight powers represented only three were properly Asiatic—the Philippines, Thailand and Pakistan; the other five were the U.S.A., Britain, Australia, New Zealand and France. What emerged was largely, but not exclusively, an American document; in form at least the pact is for mutual defence against attack from any quarter. But the omission from its text of any reference to Communism provoked an American caveat that the only form of aggression against which it would pledge itself to take immediate action was Communist aggression. Hong Kong and Formosa are areas specifically excluded from the benefits of the treaty but other countries such as Indonesia not parties to the agreement may be designated for protection if they so desire and all the signatories agree. The commitments to action are much looser than under N.A.T.O. and leave the signatories, in effect, free to determine what action they will take in the light of the circumstances obtaining at the time the treaty is invoked. The British Government, significantly, was responsible for the insertion of the proviso that "designated" territories should only be protected at their own request.

So S.E.A.T.O. began its life in vagueness and ambiguity, under American stimulus and with British acquiescence rather than positive enthusiasm. Its subsequent history has done little to increase its popularity in Britain. It has not sunk appreciably deeper roots in the life of the area. Siam, its most enthusiastic Asiatic member, has provided Bangkok for the headquarters of its Council but it cannot be said that the Council and Secretariat have been bodies with much organic vitality. The alliance has not developed military forces of its own; relying at first on Dulles's doctrine of "retaliation" by the "striking power" of American air and sea forces, it was a N.A.T.O. with no S.H.A.P.E. and all S.A.C. Initially, when the Laos crisis broke out again in 1959, it was to the U.N. rather than S.E.A.T.O. that the United States turned. Throughout, the only operative bases available to the alliance within the area have been the British base at Singapore and the American naval and air bases in the Philippines. The Americans have all along been firm in their refusal to commit land forces; the British and the other Commonwealth members have not been willing to station their forces outside the British territories in the area. Worse, S.E.A.T.O. has not been able to organize itself effectively against the Communist threat which is so much more pressing than outright war, namely subversion. It has frankly admitted that this was primarily a job for member governments themselves and that S.E.A.T.O. could only play a "supplementary" role. Since Malaya attained independence in 1957 she has evinced no desire to participate in S.E.A.T.O., though she accepted British responsibility for her external defence by a separate treaty, and she has made plain her desire that when Singapore joins Malaya S.E.A.T.O. should abandon use of the Singapore base.

All this has provoked a growing disenchantment with S.E.A.T.O. in Britain. Glad though the British Government may be to have an American "presence" in the area which throws a mantle of military protection over her remaining possessions and Commonwealth connections there, doubt has increased as to whether the form given to this American assistance is not more harmful than helpful. Some of the American aid given bilaterally to individual members has been used to feed local rivalries; it has intensified the ill-feeling between Pakistan and India over the Kashmir dispute. Much of the aid seems, even militarily, to have been wasted; worse, dollars spent on arms have not been available for the economic development which many people think should have the highest priority.[1] Though no one in the British Government has claimed a right to tell Washington how it should allocate its Asian aid, the poor returns on American investment in countries like Cambodia and Laos have not heightened respect for American policy.

For all these reasons the time seemed ripe when the Kennedy administration took over from President Eisenhower for a re-examination of American policy in the area. There was concern at the high cost of American aid for the seemingly low returns obtained, there was a waning of belief in massive retaliation and a heightened awareness of the challenge of subversion. There was even some willingness to accept the validity of neutralism as a

[1] For an incisive American statement of this position see W. W. Rostow, *The U.S. in the World Arena*, pp. 326–8.

posture for South-East Asian states. But there was also a powerful sense of frustration and a growing feeling of concern that the Communists were on the point of scoring a break-through. These diverse elements were fused by the sharpening of the Laos crisis in the early months of 1961 which provoked the urgent meeting of President Kennedy and Mr. Macmillan at Key West in March. There were relics here of the disagreements of seven years before. The British favoured the revival of the Geneva International Control Commission; the Americans were more sceptical. The British believed in the practicability and desirability of a neutral Laos; the American emphasis fell on the value of a tough warning to Moscow and Peking. At the S.E.A.T.O. Council meeting which immediately followed argument seemed to run along these lines and the communiqué which emerged, hinting at "whatever action [the members deemed] appropriate" if effort at an acceptable settlement failed, was said to represent a compromise between the "tough" and the "mild" approaches. But beneath these surface appearances there seems to have been a ground swell which was producing a real modification of American policy. When Kennedy and Khruschev met at Vienna in June the neutralization of Laos was, apparently, the one tangible agreement to be registered between them, although by the early months of 1962 Americans were complaining with some justice that the Pathet Lao treated "neutralization" as a cloak for infiltration. Even so, the Geneva Conference was re-animated in July and the "three Princes" of Laos did conclude an agreement which gave some promise of stability. It is a matter for speculation whether this could have come about had there not been a simultaneous show of allied strength in Siam. Actually the strength displayed was mainly American; when Siam in May, 1962, requested S.E.A.T.O. assistance it was the United States which responded with 5,000 troops; New Zealand and Australia sent only token contingents and the United Kingdom only a squadron of jet fighters. Even less was Britain involved when in the autumn of 1961 the decision was taken in Washington to commit American strength to South Vietnam. The process of stiffening local resistance by economic aid, the provision of arms and instructors and finally by the establishment in February, 1962, of an outright U.S. Military Command was as exclusively American in Vietnam as similar action in Malaya had been British.

8

THE MIDDLE EAST

THERE is perhaps no region of the world in which the position and interests of Britain and the U.S.A. *vis-à-vis* each other have so changed as in the Middle East. In 1938 Britain dominated the area; she held mandates in Palestine and Transjordan and effective control of Egypt, Iraq, the Red Sea and the Persian Gulf. The U.S.A. not only had no military position in the area; she had no political position there either. Her presence was either philanthropic, as in the field of missionary activity or the analogous field of higher education, or else economic. "Economic" here principally meant the development of the oil resources of the region, where American private enterprise had taken the dual form of securing a share in British or European dominated concerns, like the Iraq Petroleum Company, or of securing separate concessions such as those enjoyed by the Arabian-American Oil Company and the Bahrain Petroleum Company in the Persian Gulf.

As a corollary of this the Middle East was essentially a British theatre in World War II. The role played there by British arms reflected alike the importance of the area in British strategy and the dominance there of the existing British military and political establishment. Only in Persia, where the traditional expertize of the United States Army Corps of Engineers gave a virtuoso display of its abilities in the construction of the supply route from the Gulf to Russia, did the U.S.A. have much of a part to play.

But by 1960 the national roles had been strikingly reversed. British political control was confined to the small group of Trucial sheikdoms which bordered the Persian Gulf and, of course, to Aden. Only two British military bases remained in the area—those in Cyprus and Aden. (There is also a small garrison at Bahrain.) The U.S.A. meanwhile had advanced to a position of eminence throughout the Middle East. True, she had no territorial possessions and was nowhere accorded any formal position as a protecting power. But she had acquired bases in Turkey, Libya and Saudi

Arabia for the use of her Strategic Air Command,[1] while her Sixth Fleet in the Mediterranean made it possible for her to deploy marines and carrier planes in the Levant. Her position as a Middle East military power was formally recognized by her membership in the Military Committee of the Central Treaty Organization (C.E.N.T.O.) and by the bilateral defence agreements which she signed in 1959 with Iran, Pakistan and Turkey. Above all her economic power was felt throughout the region, not merely in the normal processes of trade and investment, but even more directly through extensive programmes of economic and military aid.

This reversal of roles by Britain and the United States was not the result of any sustained design on either side. Nor was it accomplished with much grace or suavity. Indeed, over the Suez issue in 1956 it precipitated the sharpest break in the history of the Anglo-American alliance. It represented on one side the reluctant surrender of a historic suzerainty and on the other the reluctant assumption of an uncertain responsibility. Within each country opinion was sharply divided about the course which national policy in the Middle East ought to follow and in the taking of many of the principal decisions passion and sentiment played a dangerous part. As a result the path of Anglo-American relations in the Middle East has been thickly strewn with paradoxes. When the war ended the British were sponsors of Arab unity, criticized by American Jewry for their resistance to the full realization of Zionist aspirations in Palestine. By 1956 they were accomplices after, if not before, the fact in the Israeli attack on Egypt, while the United States was supporting Egypt and the Arab world against the almost isolated trio of Britain, France and Israel. When British ascendancy in Jordan ended in 1956 with the dismissal of General Glubb from his command of the Arab Legion this was generally regarded in the U.S.A. as the overdue termination of a colonialist anomaly. Yet little more than twelve months later British parachute troops returned to Jordan under the auspices of the Sixth Fleet and the Eisenhower Doctrine.

Contradictions of this sort flowed naturally, of course, from the internal chaos of the Middle East itself, from its lack not merely of any unity but even of clear internal lines of division. Where so much was fluid, where the units of government were so numerous

[1] Though one of these, Dhahran, in Saudi Arabia was due to be given up when its lease expired in 1962.

105

and so arbitrary, where the social structure was so precarious and the administrative structure so fragile, alignments were inevitably shifty and changeable and to some extent great external powers could be excused if their policies within the area also lacked continuity and consistency. They could less easily be excused for not making up their own minds about what they wanted and for not co-ordinating their policies each with the other. The history of Anglo-American relations in the Middle East is a history of two great powers educating themselves the hard way, by making costly mistakes and by allowing pride and prejudice to become substitutes for reason and enlightened self-interest. It is not our purpose to follow that history through all its involutions, but since the present position of the United Kingdom and the United States in the Middle East is largely a product of the past, something must be said of it.

Although the Middle East has changed a good deal in the last two decades, enough has remained the same to enable one to speak of certain continuing British and American interests in the area. The oldest British interest in the Middle East arose from its position athwart the line of communication to India and other British possessions on the Indian and Pacific Oceans. Of this the classic expression was the British interest in and part ownership of the Suez Canal. With the emancipation of India, Burma and Ceylon and the development of air transport it might be thought that the traditional interconnexion of British world power and control of the Canal was largely outmoded. This might be so, were it not that in the twentieth century a new British (and indeed European) dependence developed upon oil supplies from the Middle East. For economical delivery the Canal route was virtually indispensable —at least until the development of pipe lines from the Persian Gulf to the Mediterranean, arteries which, however, had a special vulnerability of their own. And just as the importance of the Canal made it necessary for Britain to maintain a close concern in the politics of Egypt, so the importance of Middle East oil supplies gave her a similar concern in the politics of the great oil producing countries of Iran, Iraq and the Persian Gulf and Saudi Arabian areas. As far as Britain was concerned, the stability of all these states, in varying proportions, was menaced from two directions— from without and within. The great external threat came from the U.S.S.R.; it was consequently her historic and continuing endeavour to keep Russia from expanding beyond the Black Sea, the Caucasus and the Caspian and to maintain in the states which were the legatees of the Ottoman Empire a firm front against Russian pressure. Internally, the same weaknesses, political and economic, which had made it possible for the West, in the first instance, to dominate the Middle Eastern states, made them unstable and restless, wracked by mutual rivalries and a prey to powerful nationalist jealousies and aspirations. Britain's aim here was always the same —a friendly stability, but the preferred devices for securing stability varied from place to place and from time to time. They might involve a direct assumption of British political control, they might take the form of bolstering a traditional and conservative régime, they might seek to forestall revolutionary upheavals by aiding local programmes of reform and economic betterment. By the 1940's and 1950's the third alternative was most generally preferred, but often almost unavoidable recourse continued to be had also to the second, generally in conjunction with it; the first survived, only to a very limited degree, in the Trucial states of the Gulf.

There was nothing in these Middle East interests of Britain which the United States could not reasonably endorse. So as long as the strength of her European allies was important to the United States, Britain's concern with maintaining access to Middle East oil supplies might be said to be identical with America's own. The U.S.A. had no interest in expanding exports of American oil to Europe; individual oil firms might be glad to do so, but the national interest as a whole was better served by conserving the U.S.A.'s indigenous oil resources and investing American dollars in the ownership of oil wells in the Middle East, where the costs of extraction and refining were so much lower than in the United States. So although over individual concessions and upon certain occasions commercial rivalry might develop between British and American oil concerns—rivalry which might even extend to the backstairs of local politics—there was no clash of basic national interests here. Still less was it true, as conspiracy-mongers sometimes liked to make out, that there was an unholy alliance of State Department and American oil interests to undermine the British position in the Middle East.

Similarly the U.S.A.'s acute concern about the world-wide menace of Russian communism gave her every reason to support the British policy of keeping Russia out of the whole Middle

Eastern area. Indeed it was, in a sense, in this area—at least in the important Turkish sector of it—that she had first tried out her role as inheritor of the *Pax Britannica,* by the Truman Doctrine of 1947. And the U.S.A., no less than Britain, recognized the need for stability in the Middle East and the dual set of threats, internal and external, which the area had to meet.

These basic identities of interest have provided and still provide the foundation for a vital Anglo-American partnership in this part of the world. Yet they have not prevented recurrent and serious divergencies—and even outright clashes—between Britain and the U.S.A. in the Middle East. To what are these due?

The explanation must be sought on several planes. In the first place there is what one might call the different intensity of involvement. Though British and American interests here are broadly identical, the British are rooted in a deeper and, to them, more vital historical experience while at the same time coming closer to their day to day concerns as a nation. For nearly two hundred years the Middle East has taken prime place in the thinking of British policy-makers. In the crucial year of 1940 when invasion directly threatened Britain's island security it was to the Middle East that the Cabinet, without one dissenting voice, had decided to dispatch nearly half the army's best available tanks; the frontiers of Britain, not for the first time, were felt to rest upon the Nile. Here was, so to say, Britain's Panama. To the U.S.A., by contrast, the Middle East meant nothing; even the United States Marines, ranging from "the halls of Montezuma", had only reached as far as "the shores of Tripolee". The American gateway to the East was by way of her own west; more nearly perhaps than any other patch on the map, the area between Suez and Karachi was to an American the other side of the world. Thus territories which to British politicians were soused in the dangerous imponderables of national tradition, pride and sentiment, were to American policy-makers arid deserts over which "area specialists" manipulated their divining wands. For one component element in the American "nation of nations" and for one only did the Middle East have a powerful emotional significance, the Jews.

The support for the Zionist cause amongst American Jewry, though by no means universal, was sufficiently sustained, intense and focused to guarantee that *ceteris paribus* the Jewish case in Palestine would take priority over all other considerations in the

108

framing of American Middle Eastern policy. A peculiarly explosive force was lent to Zionist propaganda by the ghastly fate of European Jewry before and during World War II, and also, though sometimes subconsciously, by their anomalous position in American life, half assimilated, half rejected, at once keepers of the American conscience and strangers within the gate. The pressure thus generated was crucial at certain stages in American Middle Eastern policy, as in the refusal to implement the recommendations of the Anglo-American Palestine Committee of 1946 and the lightning recognition by Mr. Truman of the new State of Israel in 1948. Even so, it did not succeed in introducing a consistency or continuity, however partisan, into American policy; the net product, rather, was conspicuous for erraticism and contradiction, as when the U.S.A. in 1948 suddenly and belatedly abandoned partition in favour of a United Nations trusteeship which she would do nothing to implement. Whether any harmony between an American-supported Zionism and a Bevin-directed British mandate could ever have been attained is doubtful, but certainly the oscillations and reversals in American policy, as first one consideration and now another assumed dominance, created a maximum of friction and confusion.

In a sense it was true, as American Zionists claimed, that it was the inherent justice of their cause, the validity of their claims to "self-determination", to a "homeland", to become a nation like other nations, which won them their American support. Yet it was also true that this support was not able to grow roots in any soil of American national interest; American support for Zionism was the generous (even sometimes the guiltily conscientious) supererogatory action of a rich and powerful nation. As such, it had about it some of the irresponsibility that attaches to a whim; the unpredictability also, as became apparent when in 1953 the Democratic administrations which had fostered Israel were succeeded by a Republican one which was cooler to the arguments and pressures of American and world Jewry. The result within less than four years was an astonishing reversal of roles—a Britain which aided (if it did not inspire) an Israeli assault on Egypt and a U.S.A. which denounced its oldest allies and its youngest foster-child amidst the plaudits of the Arab world.

For the full explanation of this paradox we must however look less to Washington than to London. The intensity of involvement which Britain felt in the Middle East led her to an unquestioning persistence in certain beliefs and attitudes that no longer made sense there. From the point of view of her own national interest she greatly over-estimated the importance of maintaining physical control of the area. In the abstract, no doubt, it was still good to have bases from which British strength and influence could radiate. In practice, however, if those bases proved so unpopular to the countries in which they were situated that their maintenance taxed British strength and stimulated hostility to British influence, their existence became self-defeating. Moreover, with the abdication of the British Raj the great historic justification for Middle East bases, the maintenance of the lines of control to India, disappeared. There remained, of course, the two other tasks—the continued exclusion of Russsia from the area and the continuance of access to Middle East oil. For both of these a British military "presence" was certainly helpful—but only if it could be maintained without alienating local sentiment, a consideration repeatedly overlooked in country after country. Moreover, it was too readily assumed that in order to obtain Middle East oil it was necessary to own the concessions and even to control the countries from which it was obtained; by the fifties there were already signs of that world surplus of oil which afforded the best guarantee that the Middle East would continue to supply what Europe would continue to require—ample oil at reasonable prices.

It cannot be contended that the United States was entirely free of these illusions or entirely innocent of such assumptions. It was President Eisenhower who assured Sir Anthony Eden in March, 1953, that it was essential for Britain to maintain the base in Egypt and that if Britain were to evacuate the Canal Zone before making a Middle East defence arrangement she would be exposing herself to Egyptian blackmail.[1] In certain areas, for example Saudi Arabia, she judged it every bit as much in her own interests to lend her support to autocratic régimes that hardly represented the wave of the Arab future. Her especial concern as the arch-organizer of the anti-Communist front the world over sometimes led her to see Middle East countries, factions and policies exclusively in terms of a pro- or anti-Communist alignment. But in general she was free in the Middle East of the particular historic illusions of imperialism. In principle, at least, she was sympathetic to the rising tide of

[1] Eden, op. cit., p. 249.

nationalism. In specific situations this did not necessarily result, unfortunately, in her being able to offer helpful assistance or propound a practicable solution, since the disinterestedness which gave her a ready enough grasp of general principles was the reverse side of the coin of non-involvement which denied her, in many cases, a sound empirical judgement of actual situations. (This, for example, was painfully apparent over the whole Suez affair in 1956.) *Si jeunesse pouvait, si vieillesse savait.* Moreover even when she had the sympathies, she lacked in this area, time and time again, the sense of responsibility, the willingness to see through the consequences of her own recommendations and actions. The United Kingdom, by contrast, charged with a responsibility which on the whole she seldom tried to evade, all too often found herself inextricably tangled in the toils of her own historic but now erroneously conceived self-interests.

At an early stage—as early indeed as the establishment of the Middle Eastern Supply Centre during the war—some reliance began to be placed on economic and technical aid as the solvent which would melt the age-old enmities, the internecine rivalries and the nationalist suspicions of the Middle East. If only an improved economy could be established, the instabilities of the social order would be reduced and so the reliance of local governments on fraud and corruption, their susceptibility to every gust of popular passion or every touch of internal or external intrigue and subversion might be ended. Then political problems which had proved intractable in themselves might be solved indirectly by the removal of the economic and social evils which had provoked them.

British in origin, such an approach was no less attractive to the United States. It accorded with long-established American philanthropic interests in the Levant and appealed to every American policy-planner who wished to improve the stability of the area without having to incur the odium and the hazards of establishing an American political or military presence there. In Israel American capital showed what could be done to raise the productivity of one of the most arid Middle Eastern territories; if the Arab states could be aided to do half as much, the improvement in their living standards would be phenomenal. Between 1951 and 1956 the United States provided $250 million for development and technical co-operation to Israel and $86 million divided between Egypt, Iraq, Jordan, Lebanon and Saudi Arabia.

111

Unfortunately the sheer scale of Middle East under-development made any duplication of the Israeli scale of investment impossible. Outside Palestine, there were two types of underdeveloped territory, each presenting problems of their own. Superficially more fortunate were those states whose oil revenues afforded a considerable investment surplus, either in sterling or dollars. Here the problem was not one of providing the funds, but of inducing the local governments to employ them productively rather than in contributing to the conspicuous waste of their ruling families or the military under-pinning of a reactionary dynasty or, worst of all, the financing of feuds with neighbour states. In curbing such intemperances the representatives of what was known to be the richest power on earth were not always at an advantage.

The other Middle East states whose subsoil lacked these fluid riches were more straightforwardly dependent upon the U.S.A. or Britain for the wherewithal of their economic development. Here in theory the donor could dictate the uses of his gift and see that it was not wasted, nor politically perverted, nor reconverted from ploughshares into machine guns, or from tractors into tanks. Practice, however, often made nonsense of theory and local inefficiency, corruption or political necessity often made hay of the planners' hopes. In any case to secure a good return upon the investment of economic and technical aid it was necessary to have available a far larger number of skilled administrators with local knowledge than the U.S.A. could possibly supply.

Partly because of the difficulties of administering the programme efficiently in purely economic terms, partly because of the need to have something to show to Congress for its annual appropriations, the temptation became irresistible to conceive the economic aid programme in narrowly anti-Communist terms—i.e. to shift from a concern for Middle East development *per se* to an urgent desire to build up the Middle East against Communism. The result was twofold—first, to lend a readier ear to requests for military, as opposed to economic, aid from those who could present themselves as staunchly anti-Communist, even though this aid, when obtained, often increased the armaments competition and so the internal instability of the area; secondly, to require of would-be recipients of economic aid a positively pro-western proclivity which seldom accorded with their real desire, which was to stay out of the Moscow-Free World conflict and cultivate their national identities.

For all these reasons Britain found that, invaluable as American economic aid was, time and time again, in turning the tricky political corners of the Middle East, it was almost as much a source of problems as a solvent of them. The United States' failure to evolve a consistent philosophy of economic aid meant that its biggest asset in the struggle to achieve its purposes in the Middle East was not only often wasted but sometimes even recoiled upon itself.

To sum up then, three main factors underlay Anglo-American differences and difficulties in the Middle East—the different intensities of interest in the area, the persistence in Britain of outworn attitudes towards it, and the lack of any sustained philosophy of economic aid. Diplomacy, however, is not made up of general principles but of actions, often cumulative, in particular situations and to see how Britain and the United States could in one case succeed and in another fail to maximize their common interests and transcend their mutual Middle Eastern suspicions and miscalculations it may be helpful to look at two concrete instances—the Anglo-Iranian oil dispute and the Suez affair. The story of each is sufficiently well known to make a re-telling unnecessary; my object is merely to analyse some aspects of it from the distinctive point of view of their significance for the Anglo-American relationship.

The two cases had a good deal in common. In each the major interest involved was British (or Anglo-French), but in each the American role was vital. In each the dynamic element was provided by the explosive force of a local nationalism and it was on an external and so-called "imperialist" preserve that it vented itself. Over each affair loomed the presence of the U.S.S.R., not as an active but as a potential participant. On both occasions the issue was brought to the bar of world judgment, in the first case through the Security Council and the World Court, in the second through the Security Council and General Assembly.

But there were differences too and it was these, as will become apparent, which accounted for the divergent outcome. To take the Anglo-Iranian dispute first:

At the outset, in 1951, there was not much in common between the British and the American view of the issues. An affronted and expropriated Britain was convinced that she was entitled to full American support in her conflict with Mosaddeq both because her cause was just and because both countries had a common interest in maintaining the flow of Iranian oil, in resisting what was variously called "theft" or "unilateral denunciation", and in pre-venting Iran's domination by a nationalist figure or faction strongly hostile to the west. In fact the American attitude was initially cool and even critical; no direct American interest was threatened by the seizure of Anglo-Iranian; a different on-the-spot assessment was made of Mossadeq's brand of nationalism, with the result that a major American fear was that being tough with his movement would open the door to Communism in Iran,[1] finally, even where the legal merits of the British case won acceptance, there was a certain distrust of the plaintiff based upon his numerous previous convictions for colonial and imperialist malpractices. The result was that not only did the U.S.A. make strong representations just before the withdrawal from Abadan against any reclamation of British property by force; even two years later, in September, 1953, it was reported that the State Department had been urging Ameri-can oil companies to combine to buy out Anglo-Iranian.[2] From all this it might have been supposed that the prospects of Anglo-American co-operation in an agreed solution were slender. Yet in fact thesis and antithesis worked themselves out to a harmonious synthesis. Why?

In the first place the United States came by degrees to recognize that Britain had a good case, especially after the United Kingdom had appealed both to the Security Council and to the World Court; though both bodies declined to accept jurisdiction in the dispute, the result of appearing before them was in each case to present the United Kingdom in the light of one seeking justice and Iran as one reluctant even to allow the case to be heard. Secondly, the United Kingdom did eventually succeed in persuading first the Truman and then the Eisenhower administration that Mossadeq was not the only alternative to Communism in Iran. In this no doubt they were assisted by his own unreasonable behaviour but also ultimately by the demonstration provided by General Zahedi and the Shah that Mossadeq's overthrow was not the prelude to a popular wave of Communism. Thirdly, Britain abstained, despite severe temptation, from the use of force to settle the dispute, and made a continuous effort, despite intermittent friction and changes of government on both sides of the Atlantic, to work closely with the United States.

[1] Cf. President Eisenhower's remark to Eden that "he regarded him as the only hope for the West in Iran": Eden, op. cit., p. 212.

[2] Ibid., p. 214.

Fourthly, the United States was willing to accept a considerable role not merely in the negotiations but also in the settlement, both by participating in an Anglo-American marketing consortium for Iranian oil and, hardly less important, by "sweetening" the final stages of the negotiations with substantial dollar aid; over 127 million dollars of grants and loans were provided for the interim period before oil revenues from the new consortium became available. Finally, in the later phases of the dispute there was intimate co-operation between the men on the spot, the British and American ambassadors in Teheran, Sir Roger Stevens and Mr. Loy Henderson.

The result was thus the translation of the Anglo-American community of Middle Eastern interests into concrete terms. The supply and flow of oil to Europe were preserved. The independence of Iran as a bastion against the U.S.S.R. was maintained without any semblance of a *diktat* at the hands of a browbeating Western imperialism. Her economy, so utterly dependent on oil revenues, was sustained even if it was not properly stabilized (an operation necessarily the work not of a year but of decades).

The Suez affair was both shorter and sharper than the Anglo-Iranian dispute, but it was in fact (if not in form) the culmination of an Anglo-Egyptian tension which had been mounting at least since the war. So axiomatic was the British assumption that a base in Egypt was necessary to guard the Canal that the United States at various times came almost to the point of believing it too. Especially since the Truman Doctrine in 1947 London had pressed on Washington the argument that the United States and the United Kingdom had a joint defence responsibility for the Eastern Mediterranean and that for its proper discharge this responsibility required a base that safeguarded the Canal. But the American policy which issued in the Truman Doctrine stopped at the boundaries of Turkey. The U.S.A. was not willing to enter into binding mainland commitments beyond; the air bases at Wheelus and Dhahran were conceived of exclusively in S.A.C. terms, as springboards for retaliatory attacks on the U.S.S.R. And although an Eisenhower might make private expressions of endorsement of the British strategical assumptions over Suez, as in his remarks to Sir Anthony Eden quoted on p. 110, these were not translated into public statements of United States policy. Rather the reverse: not only was Mr. Dulles, as Sir Anthony Eden remarks, much less "clear and firm" on this point, but when at a certain stage a plan was put forward for

American participation in an Egyptian defence base it broke down because of Egyptian refusal to have American participation, American refusal to take part unless with Egyptian agreement and finally, as Sir Anthony Eden puts it, American reluctance "to put any pressure upon the Egyptians" to negotiate.[1]

Before 1956, of course, the vexed question of a base on Egyptian soil had been settled—on Egyptian terms. The reluctance of the Americans to press British claims against Egyptian wishes meant that all hope of maintaining an unpopular foothold had to be abandoned and undoubtedly the gradual withdrawal of British troops from the base by the treaty of 1954 was generally welcomed in the U.S.A. as a wise winding up of an imperialist legacy. To that extent Britain entered on the Suez dispute, in American eyes, with clean hands. If the odour of "colonialism" was harder to eliminate from Britain's dealings with Egypt than with Iran, she had, however belatedly, withdrawn an unwelcome presence and the Egypt which chose to expropriate British and French property in the Canal was a sovereign power with whom both the United Kingdom and the United States treated on terms of equality. Compared with the Iranian seizure, the nationalization of the Canal came nearer to touching American interests—directly because some American oil also flowed through its banks and indirectly by reason of the painful analogy to the position of Panama. Moreover the act of nationalization bore every evidence of having been precipitated, not by any British or French misdemeanour but mainly by a reversal of American policy, the withdrawal of the promised aid for the Aswan Dam.

Thus far, at the outbreak of the dispute, the omens for a harmonious Anglo-American response were, if anything, more propitious than they had been at Abadan in 1950. But two countering factors were also present from the start. The first was that long historic residue of involvement in the Canal which made its seizure such a peculiarly sensitive matter for British national pride. Everything associated with the area from Disraeli to the recollections of every ex-serviceman who wore an Africa Star guaranteed that Nasser's action would provoke an especially prickly response. And it was an exclusive response. Owing something to Lord Cromer and perhaps even more to that long line of Englishmen who have written enormous volumes of beautiful prose bound in golden buckram about their spiritual adventures in the Levant, the convic-

[1] Eden, op. cit., p. 253.

tion was general that "we could handle this"—i.e. handle it best
alone. A dangerous illusion at any time, this operated with particularly harmful consequences in 1956 by reason of the second
element present at Suez, which had been absent at Abadan. This
was the deterioration in the personal relationships of the principal
managers of the Anglo-American alliance, Mr. Dulles and Sir
Anthony Eden. At Suez the antipathy and irritation generated by
their disagreements over the Japanese Treaty, the Chinese question,
Indo-China and Geneva, E.D.C. and Western European Union had
accumulated to a point where mutual distrust was a normal characteristic of their relationship. The retirement in Britain of Sir
Winston Churchill, with his sensitive over-riding awareness of the
primacy of the Anglo-American relationship, and President Eisenhower's increasing willingness to confide in the wisdom of his
Secretary of State left no effective restraints upon the free and
baneful play of temperament on temperament. As Mr. James
Reston remarked in this connexion : "There has seldom been a
period in modern history when personality has played so large a
part in so many unhappy world events."

All the same, one thought at the time, whatever the difficulties
in the way of Anglo-American agreement, the over-arching importance of presenting a combined front to Russian pretensions
would surely, as in Iran, enforce co-operation. It should have. Why
did it fail to? Largely because the U.S.A. did not accept the British
assessment of the Soviet threat latent in the Nasser operation.
Relying on the Northern tier of anti-Soviet defences, from Istanbul
to Karachi, the Americans were a good deal less disturbed about
what the Russians might do through Nasser than they had been
about what they might do in Iran. The British could not succeed in
persuading Washington that Nasser was a mere Soviet stooge, or
even that like Mossadeq he was an absurd, unrepresentative figure
who could be replaced by a more Western-like leader equally if not
more acceptable to Egyptian taste. Nasser was no Mossadeq, Farouk
had been shown to be no Reza, and no Zahedi was in sight. Thus
the "Nasser must go" refrain in British policy fell on understand-
ably deaf ears in Washington, however much at moments they had
shared British feelings of irritation at his behaviour.

At Teheran the later stages of negotiations had been considerably smoothed and the forces of Iranian moderation strengthened
by the wise application of American economic aid. Over Suez

negotiations never reached the point where any similar emollient or buttress might be invoked. On the contrary. The efficient cause of the whole imbroglio had been the abrupt withdrawal of proferred American aid in circumstances which could be regarded, reasonably or not, as a rebuff to national pride. A clearer concept of what economic aid could achieve and a more consistent policy in its deployment might have averted the whole crisis and would at least have given the West an advantageous position for negotiation.

Although over Suez, as over Abadan, the British had taken their case before the United Nations, it had profited them less as far as the United States was concerned. To some extent this may have been because the employment of other machinery, such as the Users' Conference (at American instigation), had to some extent obfuscated the issue. But basically it was because before her appeal to the Security Council, as after it, British was insistent upon her right to resort to force if she could not get an acceptable remedy for her grievances by any other way. If at certain early stages in the dispute the President or his Secretary of State might have appeared to condone this, there could be no room for any illusions remaining in Britain about the deep repugnance this would arouse in Washington once Sir Anthony had received President Eisenhower's message of 3 September. The failure to heed this as marking the *ne plus ultra* of American co-operation was perhaps the turning-point in the diplomacy of the alliance. From then on, in place of the close consultation and co-operation that had marked the Iranian negotiations, there was an increasing breakdown of communications, in Cairo, Washington and London—not to mention Paris and Jerusalem. If in the early stages heavy blame attached to Mr. Dulles for deviousness, uncertain counsel, inopportune and ill-considered statements—in general for that something-less-than-frankness which throughout marred his diplomacy—it is certain that from this time onwards the United Kingdom, under Sir Anthony Eden, embarked upon a conspiracy with one ally, France, to the deliberate exclusion and deception of the other, the United States. Such a conspiracy when it erupted in violence and war would inevitably lead to an open breach between London and Washington.

So irrational is this cross-channel conspiracy in the context of the transatlantic community that even when all the known explanations are to hand they still seem inadequate to explain it. Ultimately they boil down to one, that the leaders of France and Britain at the time believed that there were vital national interests at stake which their partner in the transatlantic alliance was refusing to treat seriously. In their assessments of those interests they were largely wrong, as their critics told them at the time and as subsequent events have largely proved. But right or wrong, what seems most incredible of all is their belief that by acting as they did they would advance those interests more than they would harm them. The basis for this illusion was a series of gross miscalculations. They miscalculated their own military effectiveness and they miscalculated the reaction of the United States. Injured innocence is a deceptive counsellor; statesmen who rely on its exclusive advice seldom remedy their injuries and frequently impair their innocence.

It is hardly possible for a British observer, even an opponent of Suez, to provide an objective assessment of whether the American administration went too far in the "sanctions" which they applied to the United Kingdom after the outbreak of hostilities in Egypt. Their reported insistence at the United Nations upon the least accommodating resolutions and the most exacting compliance, the Vice-President, Mr. Nixon's, boast of an American "declaration of independence" from "colonialism", the pressure against sterling in the American market, the delays in the provision of emergency oil supplies for the western hemisphere, the suspension of all diplomatic contacts in Washington, the President's refusal, however reluctant, to entertain a visit from Eden until after the withdrawal of British troops from Egyptian soil—whether the line of policy thus exemplified represented the truest wisdom must be left to others to judge. It certainly represented the lowest point in Anglo-American relations of the whole post-war period.

That the Suez falling-out should so quickly have been followed by the promulgation in January, 1957, of the Eisenhower Doctrine was logical enough. Once the Franco-British venture had failed, a vacuum of power became apparent in the Middle East which had to be filled by the U.S.A. if it was not to be filled by the U.S.S.R. As such, the Doctrine was welcomed in London, though the joy there was rather of the kind that is reserved for the sinner who has repented. Ever since the idea of a Middle East defence system had been first mooted in 1951 there had been expectations, hitherto always frustrated, of American participation. Visiting the area in 1953 Dulles had aired the concept of a "northern tier" system to embrace the countries directly bordering on the U.S.S.R. But when, from this inspiration, the Baghdad Pact developed apace, Britain found that her American partner was not prepared to follow through. There was in this matter a significant reversal of the attitudes which had prevailed over S.E.A.T.O. Now it was the British who were pressing for an anti-Communist pact, even if it meant leaving out many countries of the region, and it was the Americans who were most worried about the effects on local neutrals, in this case particularly Egypt and Saudi Arabia. The Americans did not oppose it, any more than the British had opposed S.E.A.T.O.; indeed they gave arms to Pakistan and Iraq in an encouraging way. But they felt none of the urgency which Britain derived from the loss of the Suez base and the fear that, without the Pact, she might lose her military footing in Iraq when the Treaty of 1930 ran out in 1957. So, despite the persuasions that Sir Anthony Eden exercised on President Eisenhower when he visited Washington in January, 1956, the most that the U.S.A. would do, before Suez, was to join the economic and anti-subversion committees of the alliance.

Now, in place of this detachment, the Eisenhower Doctrine offered, on request, to use American forces to assist any Middle Eastern country which might be the victim of armed aggression by a state controlled by International Communism, and made this effective by offers of aid to responsive countries in the area. In Britain the way was clear for a fresh harmonization of policies. After the Macmillan-Eisenhower meeting at Bermuda in March, 1957, American participation in the military committee of the Baghdad Pact was announced. In April the swift American response to the Jordanian crisis, upholding King Hussein with the Marines and $30 million's worth of aid, showed the U.S.A. as the lineal inheritor of British policy. In the following year after the revolution in Iraq which represented a collapse of the British position there, there was the swift and co-ordinated landing of U.S. marines in the Lebanon and of British parachutists in Jordan. Whatever the wisdom or otherwise of these demonstrations in the classic style, they certainly represented an improvement in Anglo-American co-ordination since Suez. In 1959 the United States signed bilateral agreements with Turkey, Iran and Pakistan which embodied the pledges of the Eisenhower Doctrine, in rather S.E.A.T.O.-ish language, and when later in the year the Americans played host to the alliance, now renamed C.E.N.T.O., they agreed to accept the chairmanship of the military committee for 1960.

All this met with warm British approval as an indication that at last the United States was accepting firm responsibilities in a region so important to Britain and to the Commonwealth. If at Suez and immediately after there had been a suspicion that the United States was taking advantage of Britain's misfortunes to elbow her out of her position in the Middle East, this soon passed. It was now recognized that whoever was to blame in the past American strength was indispensable; moreover it gradually became apparent that Suez did not signify that extinction of British potency in the area which pessimists had at first supposed. As something of a normalization of relations even with Egypt was gradually restored, it was realized that there was still an active role for Britain to play in the life of the Middle East. It could not be played without the co-operation of the United States; but neither could it be played without the co-operation of the peoples who lived there. The problem was to find a way of securing both.

9

EUROPE: DEFENCE

ONE of the most remarkable features of Suez was the absence of any official post-mortem on the debâcle. By any normal standards—of the right or of the left, diplomatic, economic or military—it was a major national disaster. On similar occasions in the nation's past, demand for an inquest had been insistent and the resulting investigation had generally been searching. The mismanagement of the Crimean War had produced the Roebuck Committee, the bungled conspiracy of the Jameson Raid had been investigated by a select committee of the House of Commons, the tragedy of the Dardanelles had been reviewed by a Royal Commission. After Suez no inquiry was held.

This was certainly not because all the facts were known. One of the most extraordinary aspects of the affair was the secrecy which attended its preparation and the mystery which hung about it afterwards. Never in modern British history has so large an enterprise been launched in peacetime with the connivance of so few and seldom, if ever, have the lacunae in the written records been so meagrely supplemented by the oral tradition of the well-informed. Now as then, certain crucial features of the Suez imbroglio remain baffling and unprobed, and the publication by the principal actor of an apologia for his ill-starred enterprise adds substantially nothing to our knowledge of what occurred.

Not only was no inquest held. None was seriously demanded, from any responsible quarter of organized opinion. The Opposition went through the motions of calling for one, but not as men determined to get it. The reason was indeed only too obvious. The nation had been brought to the brink of a major disaster, of a rupture with the Commonwealth and a total alienation from the United States. A chasm had opened up at the country's feet; Britain had seen the peril of the position just in time and had instinctively drawn back from the abyss. To ask how she had got there and to arraign the guilty men would be to weaken her position still further. It would reveal blame and dissension not only within the Cabinet but also within the alliance; in the recriminations which would

122

assuredly follow the position of persons indispensable for continued leadership in Britain would be weakened; worse still, relations between Britain and the Eisenhower administration—an administration just about to embark on a second four-year term—would be wrecked in a cross-fire of charge and counter-charge. So when the physical collapse of Sir Anthony removed both the principal architect of the nation's misfortunes and the central witness for any inquisition, the public mood readily accepted chivalry as a substitute for justice and gratefully turned its gaze away from the blotted page of Suez to the new leaf being turned over by Mr. Harold Macmillan.

The new Prime Minister, nonetheless, had a difficult task to hand. He had to retreat without turning round, to reverse a policy without admitting that he was changing course, to repair an alliance without officially recognizing a rent. Never was the boasted empiricism of British conservatism given a better opportunity to show its paces. Here, however, our concern is not with his parliamentary and political management but with the substance of his policy. The heart of this is to be found in a reassertion of priorities; the unity of the Commonwealth and the maintenance of the Anglo-American alliance were to be given priority over the *entente* with France and even over the assertion of our rights and interests in traditional areas of British influence and control, like the Middle East. Fortunately—it was the saving grace of the whole Suez affair —no choice had to be made between the first two priorities; Britain's relations with the Commonwealth dove-tailed with, indeed, supported, her relations with the United States. (Never was this more conspicuously displayed than in those lonely days after the Anglo-French landings when, both in Washington and in the United Nations, it was only the other members of the Commonwealth who kept open lines of communication which, as far as direct contact between London and Washington was concerned, had been cut.) The importance which Mr. Macmillan attached to strengthening those Commonwealth bonds which Suez had so severely strained was exemplified not only at the routine Commonwealth Prime Ministers' Conference in 1957 but also by his own 20,000-mile tour of the Commonwealth in 1958, the first ever to be undertaken by a British Prime Minister while in office. The restoration of relations with the United States was conveniently symbolized in the popular image of Macmillan and Eisenhower renewing an old comradeship which went back to their wartime association in North Africa. A symbol, however, is all that it was. After all, the personal amity of old comrades-in-arms had been even more impressively symbolized in the Churchill-Eisenhower relationship which lasted from 1953 to 1955, yet these were the years in which the unity of the alliance most notably began to deteriorate. The test was whether, behind the symbolism, they could make a reality of partnership. A precondition of this was that Britain on her part should make a realistic assessment of her interests and potentialities and that the U.S.A., on hers, should remember that it was an alliance she was leading and should accept her consequential responsibilities for both consultation and decision.

Suez illuminated more than just the failure of British Middle East policy and the breakdown of her relations with her major ally. It showed up the inadequacy of her whole defence policy and called into question the scale and diversity of the commitments which the nation had been trying to shoulder. Although Britain had spent £7,000 million in five years on defence, it was now revealed that her forces were still not equipped for a comparatively simple operation and that what equipment they had was not what they needed. (It might also have been observed that the most costly of her armaments, the nuclear weapon, could not for political reasons be deployed at all.) The strain put by the Suez operations upon the national finances was a reminder that the nation was like a man with weak lungs whom the least over-exertion would find short of breath; the limits of its politico-military endeavours were set by the weakness of its monetary reserves, the least overstrain producing a run on the pound. Thus, as time and time again after World War II, the country's foreign and defence policy had to be re-examined in the light of what the economy could support. (Since, in such a plight, the only possible source of succour was from the dollar world, since in fact the financial crisis required the invocation of the waiver in the Anglo-American loan agreements, even this recutting of the national cloth involved harmonizing British policy with that of the U.S.A.) A glance at the nation's accounts revealed that if there had to be cuts the defence budget was a particularly inviting place to make them. This was for the double reason that so much defence expenditure took place overseas and that so much even of what was spent at home consumed the products and manpower of those industries, notably engineering and electronics, which were particularly needed for the export trade. It was not difficult to argue that the heavy burden of defence which Britain had carried during and since the Korean war had substantially contributed to the inflation which had undoubtedly diminished her effectiveness as a world power.

This was the thinking which was made explicit in the revolutionary Defence White Paper of 5 April, 1957, and which was invoked to justify its programme of cuts, switches and revised commitments. The White Paper virtually assumed that it was defence which would have to bear the brunt; it did not consider the possibility of cutting investment or consumption, no doubt because the first would have imperilled an already inadequate rate of economic growth and the second would have disappointed expectations nursed by both Government and Opposition. In any case the New Year that saw the withdrawal from Suez under the cover of a United Nations expeditionary force was not a season for invoking the heroic mood. The national disposition was rather to explore, with some avidity, the compensations of "leaving it to Dag".

Ten years earlier and in a related part of the world Britain had once before arrived at the conclusion that her reach had exceeded her grasp. In the Greco-Turkish crisis of 1947, a similar retrenchment having been forced upon her, she turned to the United States and persuaded her to move in in her place. Her case then for relief as a war-weary, austerity-ridden partner was in many ways better founded in 1947 than it was in 1957 when she was floundering in difficulties largely of her own making. Yet paradoxically the Britain of Macmillan and Selwyn Lloyd seems to have found in Washington a readier acceptance of her desire to cut commitments than did the Britain of Attlee and Ernest Bevin. By 1957, without doubt, the United States had become only too painfully cognisant of the recurrent problem of Britain's balance of payments and hardly needed much convincing as to the limitations set by our inflation-prone economy. Moreover if the "New Look" in British defence policy was at any time queried in Washington its British advocates could claim with some justice that they were only following a precedent which the Eisenhower administration had laid down.

The Eisenhower new look had its basis in the contention—almost identical with that of the British White Paper—that, as the President insisted in his State of the Union message in January, 1953, "adequate military strength" must be achieved "within the limits of an endurable strain" on the economy. Rooted in this conviction of the dependence of military power on a balanced budget, the disposition to cut the United States defence expenditure was stimulated by the sunnier international prospect that opened with the death of Stalin and the ending of the Korean War. Technologically, the demonstration of the annihilating power of the hydrogen bomb at the Eniwetok explosion in November, 1952, encouraged the belief that the immense destructive power of nuclear weapons would provide the all-purpose answer to the needs of defence. The result was the emergence, at the point where defence and diplomacy meet, of the doctrine of "massive retaliation" which received its most challenging enunciation at the hands of Mr. Dulles on 12 January, 1954:

> "Before military planning could be changed, the President and his advisers in the National Security Council had to take some basic policy decisions. This has been done. The basic decision was to depend primarily upon a great capacity to retaliate, instantly, by means and at places of our choosing. Now the Department of Defence and the Joint Chiefs of Staff can shape our military establishment to meet the enemy's many choices. That permits a selection of military means instead of a multiplication of means."[1]

The re-shaped "military establishment" that this implied was revealed in the President's 1954 budget message with its proposals to expand the Air Force from 106 wings to 137 by mid-1957 and to reduce the Army from 3·4 million men in 1954 to 3·2 million in 1955 (further cut to 2·85 million in 1956); funds were re-allocated between the services in proportion and the 1953 expenditure of 43·6 billion dollars was to be cut to 41·5 billion in 1954 and 37·6 billion in 1955 respectively.

Some of the problems which this "new look" implied for the alliance have already been mentioned. The increased reliance upon nuclear striking power seemed to imply a set of exclusively American decisions about intervention around the globe—or, to put it another way, about when and where to turn a local "conventional" conflict into a global, atomic one. The shift from conventional to atomic forces if persisted in seemed also to imply

---

[1] *Documents on American Foreign Relations, 1954*, pp. 7–15

a re-allocation of burdens in the alliance, with the U.S.A. making her contribution mainly through the atomic deterrent plus a reserve possibly stationed in a "garrison America", while her allies manned the local ramparts and provided the bulk of manpower. Much of the alarm this aroused in Britain was based upon the all too ready assumption that every tendency will be developed to its logical conclusion; as a result, revolutionary implications were read into what was often only a shift of emphasis. But indisputably the effect of the new strategical posture was, as we have seen, to weaken the bonds of alliance both by reducing confidence in American leader- ship and by inciting similar strategies "of their own choosing" amongst other members of the alliance who thought they could afford them.

In Britain indeed a mild dose of infection had already been caught well before 1957. The 1954 White Paper envisaged a "gradual change" in the defence effort with a "tendency" to a declining expenditure on the army and "greater emphasis" on the R.A.F.; accordingly, it announced the decision to begin construction of the V-bomber force. The decision in 1955 to build a British hydrogen bomb marked a further stage in the same direction. The 1957 White Paper is however properly regarded as a new departure with its abolition of conscription by 1960 (thus cutting the army strength by 50 per cent), its immediate cut in the Rhine Army by 13,000 men with more to follow, the demotion of the Navy, and, above all, the reliance on nuclear weapons. Though its progress was to be spread over five years, its impact made itself felt immediately. Nowhere was it greater, or more painful, than in N.A.T.O.

Though the White Paper envisaged a strategy which rested almost entirely upon collective action, renouncing isolated British action in all except the most "brushfire" of operations, its immediate effect appeared to be a reduction in the British contribution to the various alliances she supported, and particularly to N.A.T.O. The decision to stop conscription, the reduction in the naval contribution to N.A.T.O. forces, the halving of the tactical air force in Germany, and, above all, the cut in the British Army of the Rhine—these all seemed to point to a weakening zeal for the North Atlantic alliance. The cut in the Rhine Army caused particular unease; only two and a half years earlier Sir Anthony Eden had secured French consent to a German army with the pledge to maintain on the continent four divisions and the tactical air force

127

and not to withdraw them "against the wishes of the majority of the Brussels Treaty powers". The powers concerned did not formally set themselves against the British decision—though they prevailed on the British government to effect a smaller reduction than that originally desired—but they made no secret of their dislike of it. For this and the other economies in their overseas defence expenditure the British could indeed produce a strong debating argument over and above the over-ruling claim of necessity. This was that throughout the fifties the United Kingdom had contributed to defence a higher proportion of her national income than any other West European country, except France, and in having to contribute most of it abroad carried its burden in a peculiarly onerous form. Nor, it was said, could France complain so long as the mass migration of the French army to Algeria left only one shadowy French division in N.A.T.O. But this kind of retort did nothing to ease N.A.T.O.'s problem as an alliance less than half equipped with even the thirty divisions which its supreme Commander had reluctantly accepted as a reduced target two years earlier. The fact of the matter was that the 1957 White Paper represented a further shift in the balance of N.A.T.O., with less emphasis on the conventional shield and more reliance on the nuclear sword. The White Paper claimed that it would be in her provision of a nuclear deterrent—the V-bomber force, missiles, the arming even of her conventional forces with nuclear weapons— that the main British contribution to collective defence would be made.

When N.A.T.O. was first established the sword on which it relied was an exclusively American one—the atom bomb, to be delivered by S.A.C. The manufacture of the weapon and the maintenance of a means of delivery were both immensely costly. Why did Britain seek to duplicate them? The answer, of course, has little to do with N.A.T.O., though much with the United Kingdom's position *vis-à-vis* the rest of the world: possession of the super-weapon seemed indispensable to the maintenance of her position as a world power. (And of course possession of the weapon demanded as a corollary capacity to deliver it.) But paradoxically the American refusal to share her own atomic secrets with the ally who had contributed most to her own atomic programme provided a supplementary stimulus, since access to American atomic secrets was restricted by the McMahon Act to allies who were also atomic

powers. Thus to enjoy the benefits of association we had first of all
to demonstrate that we "could go it alone".

This was the first great *raison d'être* for the British deterrent.
But from the outset there were supplementary ones too. From the
outset of the alliance there was always the problem of maintaining
Britain's voice in its councils when one member, the U.S.A. disposed of a strength not merely so much greater but of a wholly
different order from that of all the rest. If this power were aug-
mented by a monopoly of the super-weapon, Britain's voice might
dwindle to a whisper. To be heard, she had to be able to make a
big bang too. In a double sense this was felt to be wise. *Vis-à-vis*
America Britain had to establish her right to be consulted in all
decisions which might involve the use of the bomb. *Vis-à-vis* the
U.S.S.R. her possession of an independent deterrent entitled her to
an independent voice at Moscow and guaranteed that she would be
respected in any bilateral controversy and also gain admission to
any East-West exercises in summitry. The logic behind these arguments was something less than water-tight; the U.S.A. had a moral
obligation to consider any ally who might be involved in a decision
to use the ultimate weapon; if the U.S.S.R. decided to strike, the
smaller British sting would add little to the U.S.A.'s large one and
if the U.S.S.R. insisted on a two-man summit Britain's bomb would
not guarantee her a third seat. But the logic of these counter-
arguments was not quite water-tight either. In a world where reason
counted for less than the vague penumbra of respect inspired by
power the British deterrent seems to have secured her certain advantages in both Washington and Moscow. In Washington in particular it was Britain's status as a nuclear power which was largely
responsible for her retaining, on an informal basis, that right to
"pre-annihilation" consultation originally formally embodied in the
Quebec Agreements. More certainly, this status admitted Britain to
consultation with the Americans on contingency planning, on
target selection and the like from which she would otherwise
almost certainly have been excluded. Finally in all the East-West
negotiations, including particularly those on disarmament and
nuclear testing, it secured her a voice which she would otherwise
have been denied. This whole intangible or "prestige" value of the
deterrent found as explicit assessment as any in statements con-
secutively made by Opposition and Government leaders in the
House of Commons debate on the manufacture of the British

hydrogen bomb on 2 March, 1955. Mr. Attlee, supporting the Government's decision, said:

> "I think that we have influence in the world. That influence does not depend solely upon the possession of weapons, although I have found, in practical conversations, that the fact that we do possess these weapons does have an effect upon the rulers of other countries. It is quite an illusion to think that it does not have an effect. I am quite sure that we should not have had the influence we did have upon the events in Korea if we had not had the Commonwealth Division there."[1]

Mr. Macmillan, as Defence Minister, defended the decision in these terms:

> "It may be argued that because the main deterrent force is American there need be and there ought to be no British contribution. I think that is a very dangerous doctrine.
>
> It is doubly dangerous on two levels of thought. Politically, it surrenders our power to influence American policy and then, strategically and tactically, it equally deprives us of any influence over the selection of targets and use of our vital striking forces. The one, therefore, weakens our prestige and our influence in the world and the other might imperil our safety."[2]

But to these arguments, as "New Look" thinking developed on each side of the Atlantic, there was added another, which strikingly revealed the grim logic, the self-multiplying potency of weapons of destruction. In the May Day parade of 1954 Russians displayed the rudiments, at least, of a S.A.C. of their own; in November, 1956, they boasted in their anti-Suez note to Britain of their ability to bomb London with rockets with nuclear warheads. Thus was ushered in a new phase of strategic thinking—and worrying—in Britain, based upon the fact that the U.S.S.R. could wield a nuclear deterrent of its own. In the event of war would S.A.C. give the same priority to attacks on Soviet bases which directly threatened Britain as the V-force would? And, looking beyond this to the I.C.B.M., the Intercontinental Ballistic Missile, with its 5,000-mile

[1] HC Deb., 5th series, Vol. 537, col. 2175.

[2] Ibid., col. 2181–2.

range, what would happen when the U.S.A. and the U.S.S.R. could fire at each other direct? When United States bases were no longer needed in Britain would the U.S.A. still regard a threat to, Britain as a threat to herself? Against such a day Britain must have a deterrent of her own.[1] The trouble about this argument was that it proved too much. It envisaged the collapse of N.A.T.O. and all hope of a collective defence based on collective guarantees. If it was valid for the United Kingdom *vis-à-vis* the U.S.A. it was valid for every western European country against both the United Kingdom and the U.S.A. That way total disintegration of the alliance lay.

None of this reasoning, it will be readily apparent, could have recommended the new White Paper policy to Washington. Yet the policy itself required and obtained not merely acquiescence but even positive support from the U.S.A. Mr. Duncan Sandys' January, 1957 mission to Washington was an indispensable precursor of his April manifesto. With the V-bomber forces still on the drawing boards the whole policy of a British deterrent was dependent on the provision by the U.S.A. of the I.R.B.M.s, Intermediate, Range Ballistic Missiles, which was first negotiated by Mr. Sandys and finally clinched by Mr. Macmillan in his Bermuda talks in March. The considerations which persuaded President Eisenhower to facilitate the British "New Look" by this extra-N.A.T.O. provision have not been made public. No doubt the logic of his own "New Look" precedent counted for a good deal and the force of the "economy" argument would not have been lost on the President. There was also a general desire to do everything reasonable to make up the dissensions of Suez and to accede to any reasonable British request. There was almost certainly, on the American administration's part, a certain feeling of guilty conscience at having failed to make good on its intentions about atomic secret-sharing. Basically, however, one suspects there was a kind of live and let live philosophy not untypical of the President, which rested the alliance rather on a free co-operation of individual efforts than upon any universally accepted and rigorously worked-out strategy and allocation of functions. In a relationship so conceived something

[1] Thus Mr. Sandys to the House of Commons on 16 April, 1957: "When they have developed the 5,000 mile intercontinental ballistic rocket can we really be sure that every American administration will go on looking at things in quite the same way?" Ibid. Vol. 568, col.: 1761.

like the British "New Look" was a logical consequence of the position in which the United Kingdom found herself in 1957, with its
blend of dependence and independence of the U.S.A. She was
dependent, as Suez had demonstrated, in her inability to wage a
war of which the United States disapproved, or to stand up to
Soviet threats alone. She was independent in having manufactured,
in her ally's despite, a considerable range of nuclear weapons (the
British hydrogen bomb was exploded in May, 1957). She was
desperately anxious to avoid economic dependence on United States
aid (hence the economic motive for the defence reductions) and
equally anxious to restore, as soon as possible, the broken intimacy
of the alliance. Finally she was as determined as ever not to go
farther into Europe than her transatlantic ally. These were the ingredients which, given the American policies of the last few years,
almost dictated the British White Paper of 1957.

This was the situation when, on 4 October, 1957, the Russian
sputnik shook the West. On British-American relations this manifestation of Soviet spacemanship had two important effects. Just as
the Berlin crisis of 1948 made British bases highly desirable for
the United States strategic bombing force, so sputnik made British
bases almost indispensable for United States missile strategy. The
missile offer of the Bermuda talks now took on a new meaning as
a strengthening not only of Britain's nuclear deterrent but also of
America's nuclear defences. But, more than this, the natural desire
of the Pentagon not to put all their nuclear eggs in one basket led
to the attempt, at the N.A.T.O. meeting in December, to secure
agreements with other European allies about the deployment of
Intermediate Range Ballistic Missiles on their territories. Here,
however, a further consequence of sputnik revealed itself—a new
distrust in continental Europe of American leadership and an
enhanced desire to negotiate with Moscow before incurring the
peculiar odium which Moscow professed to reserve for countries
that accepted American missile bases. The United States proposal
was shelved until 1958.

Two months before the inconclusive N.A.T.O. meeting of
December Mr. Macmillan had met President Eisenhower in Washington for what was, in effect, a sequel to the Bermuda meeting of
March. The atmosphere of renewed amity created at Bermuda was
intensified at Washington. *The Times* reported that "in terms of
the Anglo-American alliance participants in the talks have known

nothing like them since the wartime conferences at Cairo and Casablanca".[1] The conversations concluded with a "Declaration of Common Purpose", a somewhat wordy communiqué which for British readers contained as its most significant item an undertaking by the President that he would ask Congress to amend the Atomic Energy Act to permit collaboration "between Great Britain, the United States and other friendly countries". The emphasis throughout fell indeed on "interdependence"; "national self-sufficiency" was recognized as being out of date and was to be replaced by "genuine partnership". Care was taken to stress that this was not just an Anglo-American commitment, that in fact "the understandings . . . reached will be increasingly effective as they became more widespread between the free nations". As if to symbolize this, M. Spaak, as Secretary-General of N.A.T.O., was invited to attend the final session of the conference. From the British point of view, however, the importance of the Washington meeting was as a milestone in the restored and growing intimacy of the Anglo-American relationship. As such it was hailed in London with applause which was almost more heartfelt for being determinedly unobstreperous. At last, it was felt, the ravages of Suez had really been erased and the easy, informal, frank Anglo-American "intercom." was fully in operation again.

On the continent of Europe, and particularly in France, "interdependence" was translated as "the Anglo-American directorate" and was proportionately ill-conceived. This was reflected in a demand at the N.A.T.O. meeting for a strengthening of political consultation within N.A.T.O., a demand for which France, however, failed to get significant support—largely because she interpreted consultation to mean endorsement of French policies on the N.A.T.O. periphery, Algeria in particular. But there was an indubitable drawing together of France, Germany and, to a lesser degree Italy, symbolized and fortified, immediately after the meeting, by the coming into force on New Year's Day, 1958, of the European Common Market. The political overtones of this economic alliance rang loud for all to hear. They were ringing even louder at the end of 1958 when France rejected the United Kingdom's proposal to establish instead a free trade area for the whole of Western Europe.

In February, 1958, the British-American missile agreement was

[1] *The Times*, 26 October, 1957.

made effective, with the U.S.A. supplying sixty "Thor" missiles for installation on fixed sites in eastern Britain. No other N.A.T.O. ally offered America a comparably prompt response. Indeed by the end of 1958 only Italy had become fully committed to an acceptance of these hazardous imports. (Turkey came in soon after.) France, now fortified in her angularity by General de Gaulle's assumption of power, most conspicuously declined to accept them except on terms which guaranteed an exclusively French control of the nuclear warheads. In the abstract terms of "principle" which generally only serve to advertise a plaintiff's weak position, the General was no doubt right to assert that it was a derogation of national self-respect to provide housing for the missiles of a country which would not even trust its allies with the key to their warheads. But the contrast between British indifference and French sensitivity on this score probably represented not different degrees of national pride so much as the different psychologies of an atomic and a not-yet-atomic power. As an atomically "have" nation, the British sympathized with the American concern about the dispersal of these "ultimate" weapons even to the length of being willing to forgo some of her own undoubted "rights" in their control. Unfortunately other events in 1958 contributed further to French stand-offishness.

On 3 July announcement was made of an Anglo-American agreement on nuclear weapons which at last represented that frank sharing of atomic secrets which Britain had long claimed as a right and sought as an ally. It provided for a full exchange of information about both atomic weapons themselves and about their delivery, thus making the United Kingdom at all points an equal partner with the U.S.A. in the atomic field.[1] France, working hard to make an atomic bomb of her own, was by contrast left still in the position of total exclusion which Britain had occupied down to 1954. On top of this a few days later came the Anglo-American landings in Lebanon and Syria, conducted without even token French participation. It would be hard to think of any type of action in any other area which would have so emphatically demonstrated Britain's

[1] The coping-stone was set on this revived atomic alliance in February 1962, with the joint announcement that a British nuclear device would be tested underground in Nevada and American atmospheric tests would be conducted on Christmas Island.

change of priorities within the alliance and the revival of Anglo-American intimacy.

The result was a strong Gaullist demand for the recognition of France by the U.S.A. as an alliance partner at least equivalent to Britain and for the creation of a political triumvirate within N.A.T.O. which would deal with all problems of common concern, inside Europe or without. The proposal won little support in Washington, especially since the first fruits of any such trinitarian policy-planning would surely be a French demand for full support in Algeria. Moreover, how deny to Adenauer, whose country after all was contributing seven N.A.T.O. divisions to France's one, what would be conceded to De Gaulle? For these and other reasons Washington was unresponsive. In return De Gaulle became more unco-operative. He declined to allow any of the French air force to be integrated within a West European air command and in March, 1959, withdrew from N.A.T.O. that portion of the French Mediterranean fleet (approximately one-third of the total) which had previously been under the operational control of N.A.T.O.'s C.-in-C. Africa-Mediterranean. This was followed in midsummer by a refusal to allow N.A.T.O. to station on French soil American fighter-bombers which were armed with tactical nuclear weapons.

The immediate result of such a policy was only to reinforce the links between London and Washington. Closely on the heels of the French refusal came the announcement of a N.A.T.O.-United Kingdom agreement providing for the transfer of the bulk of the two hundred fighter-bombers concerned to airfields in East Anglia (the rest being accepted by Western Germany). The promptness of the British acceptance spoke for itself. Thus even within N.A.T.O., where the 1957 White Paper had undoubtedly done more harm than good, British conduct appeared co-operative when contrasted with the stubborn self-centredness of the French.

Meanwhile the British role in the basic American strategy of her own nuclear deterrent remained. Technical development, though proceeding at an over-accelerating tempo, had still not eliminated the advantages that attached to an advanced island base. As the missile replaced the bomber the day might come when Moscow and Washington would think (and aim) only for each other, but in 1960 that day had not yet come. Indeed the first result of the development of a Russian I.C.B.M. was the creation of a new function for Britain in American defence planning; while she was still passing from being the unsinkable aircraft-carrier to being the short-range missile base she was also asked to become the early warning screen of the west. In February, 1960, agreement was reached on the construction at Fylingdales in Yorkshire of a huge radar screen which would detect missiles launched against Britain or, over Britain, against America. It was to be a joint Anglo-American project with the United Kingdom contributing £8 million of its cost to the U.S.A.'s £35 million—a division roughly proportionate to the warning times it would provide, four minutes to the United Kingdom, and fifteen minutes to the United States.[1]

Meanwhile the conviction was belatedly growing in Britain that the search for a British I.R.B.M.—"Bluestreak"—which would ultimately replace the V-bomber force was costing more than it was worth. On 13 April, 1960, Mr. Watkinson, Minister of Defence, announced its abandonment. Instead it was decided to lengthen the life of the V-bombers by equipping them with the air-borne missile "Skybolt", under design in the U.S.A. In June, on Mr. Watkinson's visit to Washington, the Americans agreed to furnish "Skybolt" when developed and to accept British participation in its development, testing and production.

The search for the invulnerable deterrent led inevitably to the sea. The development of the nuclear-powered, nuclear-armed submarine followed a familiar course—first the U.S.A., then the U.S.S.R. and then, in order of aspiration, the United Kingdom and France. Thanks however to the 1958 Agreement the British did not have to wait as long for American assistance over this as over the atomic bomb. *Nautilus*, the first American nuclear-powered submarine, was launched in January, 1954. In June, 1959, it was followed by the *George Washington*, the first such vessel designed to fire ballistic missiles. Offers of an atomic reactor suitable for driving a submarine were made to Britain as early as July, 1957, and France as early as July, 1958, but the restrictions of American law forbade the administration to follow through on the promise to France. All that she received (by an agreement signed on 7 May, 1959) was a promise of enriched uranium, spread over a ten-year period, for experimental work. By contrast the sale to

[1] A year later in July 1961 this kind of co-operation was taken a stage further by the agreement to establish a ground station in Cumberland which would take in information on missile attacks received from satellites orbiting at an altitude of 300 miles.

Britain of a complete nuclear propulsion plant was authorized on 3 July, 1958, an arrangement which materially accelerated the construction of Britain's first atomic-powered submarine, the *Dreadnought*, launched on 21 October, 1960. Meanwhile for the American *George Washington* type of submarine, whose "Polaris" atomic missiles had a range of only some 1,250 miles, a base in British waters was, though not essential, certainly extremely advantageous. In November, 1960, the agreement was announced by which a submarine would be based on Holy Loch in the Clyde, serviced by a depot ship of 18,500 tons and a small shore establishment. Thus a facility for sea, comparable to the earlier facilities for the air, became a feature of the Anglo-American partnership in nuclear deterrence.

From the beginning British governments had fully realized—and had often made public—the implications that the harbouring of the American deterrent had for British security and British relations with the iron curtain world. In 1960, however, these implications became explicit in a form which, though it left British policy unchanged, yet temporarily jolted the smooth working of the alliance and demonstrated the need for constant vigilance and the utmost clarity in the allocation of spheres of responsibility. The catastrophe of Captain Powers's U-2 flight which brought down in its wake the summit meeting of May, 1960, was nowhere felt more sharply than in Britain. No country had invested more hope or more effort in the long-contrived and quickly-concluded encounter of East and West; more practically, the secretive independence of the United States Central Intelligence Agency was suddenly realized as something that threatened the whole structure of consultation and collaboration on which the alliance rested. True, it was neither from nor to a British base that Captain Powers's plane had flown, but such comfort as could be derived from this fact was largely erased in July by the Russian claim to have shot down an RB 47 which was based in Oxfordshire. The RB 47 was almost certainly innocent of any violation of Soviet air space, but put together the two incidents added up to a comprehensive reminder of the inescapable hazards of the cold war and also of the imperative necessity of mutual trust and intimate consultation for the successful working of the alliance.

The presence and functioning of the United States air force in Britain was indeed a classic exemplification of the Anglo-American alliance at its most informal. Accepted in 1948, in immediate response to the Berlin alarm but ultimately in relation to the whole growing challenge of the U.S.S.R., the S.A.C. striking force operated from its British bases under what the Secretary of Air described to the House of Commons in March, 1951, as "informal arrangements".[1] Though of course for some matters, such as finance and the legal status of the forces, there were written agreements, the great political and strategic implications of their presence were not explored in any written document. This seems to have been the position until 18 October, 1951, when what was variously described as a "formula" and an "understanding" was arrived at between Mr. Attlee and President Truman "under which the use in emergency of bases in this country by United States forces was accepted to be a matter for joint decision in the light of circumstances prevailing at the time". But even this "depended on no formal document. It was accepted as a mutually satisfactory arrangement which was subsequently confirmed in the joint statement issued on 9 January, 1952",[2] by Mr. Churchill and Mr. Truman; this simply made public the Attlee-Truman formula in the terms quoted.

These agreements were of course in essence, as we have seen, an application to changed circumstances of the wartime Quebec Agreement about the use of the atomic bomb. As such they did indeed provide an essential safeguard for the tenants of the unsinkable aircraft-carrier in the event of war or imminent risk of war. They served also as the model for the subsequent agreements about the missile bases and the custody of the nuclear warheads. They were not, however, applicable to the other "non-emergency" operations of American aircraft based in Britain; these were left, in exactly the spirit of the 1948 agreement, to be regulated, in writing or not, by the joint decisions of the services concerned. There were advantages and drawbacks to such a system. As long as there was American hypersensitiveness about any infringement of the Mc-Mahon Act there was obviously much to be said for local arrangements, in a spirit of intra-service amity, which did not put too much down in black and white. Yet, as the U-2 and RB 47 incidents illustrated, this might lead either or both services to excesses of adventurous zeal and lead the political heads in either or both

[1] HC Deb. 5th series, Vol. 485, col. 277, 21 March, 1951.

[2] Quotations from statements by Mr. Macmillan to House of Commons: ibid., Vol. 626, col. 1176–7, 12 July, 1960.

countries into trouble for themselves and for the alliance. Some tightening up was obviously necessary and Mr. Macmillan responded to a widespread British demand by taking the matter up with Mr. Eisenhower before and during his visit to Washington in October, 1960. Security forbade any publication of the arrangements made but Mr. Macmillan reported to the House of Commons on his return that he was satisfied that they were satisfactory. "I think I can say that we are fully informed on both sides of everything that is proposed to be done."[1]

[1] Ibid., Vol. 627, col. 2146–7, 25 October, 1960. The continued validity of the Quebec agreements and their world-wide applicability were also affirmed by Mr. Macmillan in a statement in the House of Commons on 26 June, 1962: "There is an understanding which I had with President Eisenhower and now have with President Kennedy that neither of us in any part of the world would think of using power of this kind without consultation with each other."

EUROPEAN UNIFICATION

SEEN from Downing Street there are two Europes. There is the Europe of defence, which is an integral part of the whole North Atlantic region and finds its natural expression in N.A.T.O., and there is the Europe of everything else, but principally of economics—of trade, finance, communications and cultural exchanges—which has found many partial expressions but as yet none which is adequate. To Britons the distinction has seemed as natural as that between geography and history. In determining their relations with the first Europe the arguments of proximity have taken precedence over all others and bound them to a mainland only 20 miles away. In all else the bonds of Commonwealth, race, language, culture, trading habits and investment have linked them so strongly with other continents as to leave Europe as only one competitor, and that not the strongest, for their island affections and attachments.

To a high degree Washington has accepted this dual view and has operated, in its dealings with Britain on European matters, upon a roughly similar distinction. It too has viewed European defence as *sui generis* and in general, where practical issues are concerned, has found the tempo and degree of Britain's fusion with the continent fully acceptable[1]—indeed for many purposes it has found British insularity a positive advantage. But though it has accepted the pigeon-holes, it has been less satisfied with the policy it has found in them—or at least in the one labelled variously European "union", "unification" or "integration". To Britons it has never been easy to understand why, just because the Channel is narrower than the Atlantic, Americans should expect them to have an attitude to European integration so different from their own. To Americans it has always been puzzling that a country so close to Europe should on so many issues persistently remain aloof from it. The explanation can, in the main, be found in three factors.

[1] With the possible exception of the British attitude to E.D.C., for which see pp. 55 ff.

Where defence has been concerned Britain has been, since 1941 (and before), a consistently reliable ally to the United States. Indeed in the organization of West European defence British initiative has counted for as much as American. Though no N.A.T.O. member has a perfect record, Britain's role in the alliance has been that of a strong, self-reliant partner able to contribute at least as much as she receives. In other words in American eyes Britain's assessment of her place in the defence of Europe has been justified, by results; she has pursued policies which she has been able to sustain and which in the main have worked. By contrast, in the economic field Britain has been a good deal less strong and reliable. If she was a promoter of European co-operation in O.E.E.C. and E.P.U., her own persisting inflationary pressures and balance of payments deficits have weakened her role in European recovery and obliged her to lean, time and time again, upon the economic crutch of dollar aid. Thus a European role which has seemed adequate where defence is concerned has not seemed adequate in the economic and related fields. The same applies to the British insistence on a "special relationship" with Washington. Around the provision for S.A.C.'s use of reliable British bases was built both a defence for America and the N.A.T.O. shield. But the hopes of Washington planners that the Anglo-American loan agreement of 1946 would equally quickly establish an economically viable Britain which in partnership with the U.S.A. would reconstruct world trade and with it the economies of the free nations were shown to be illusory. When Britain was found unequal to this role the bilateral partnership had to be replaced by the European-American venture of the Marshall Plan.

In explaining their reluctance to enter an "integrated" Europe no factor was more often invoked by British spokesmen than the ties between Britain and the Commonwealth. Where European defence was concerned the Americans had little difficulty in recognizing the Commonwealth connexion as a source of British strength. Not only was Canada one of the pillars of N.A.T.O. but even countries like Australia and New Zealand which accepted no explicit commitments to defend Western Europe were likely, if the worst came to the worst, to stand by the United Kingdom as they had done before. True, Britain was obliged, upon occasion, to restrict her N.A.T.O. commitments because of the calls made upon

her by Commonwealth defence, and to this extent the Commonwealth connexion was a European liability, but Americans recognized the Commonwealth as a stabilizing element in the world and
consequently in general accepted this as merely the inevitable price
of Britain being a world power. However, when the issue at stake
was economic the Americans viewed the Commonwealth connexion
with more scepticism. Long before the war they had resented
imperial preference as only a country with a long protectionist tradition could; the British refusal in all the 1944–6 financial negotiations to dismantle this structure had been generally regarded as a
perverse reluctance to join the forces of light. Even the sterling
area, for all its efficacy as a trading unit, was often regarded with
suspicion as a device for insulating the City of London against the
healthy blasts of financial competition. When therefore the claims
of Commonwealth trade were invoked as a reason for staying out
of Europe the argument seldom struck a really responsive chord in
the United States.

Finally, if the British attitude towards European "integration"
won little support in Washington, the contradictoriness and
gaucherie of British public pronouncements must carry a lot of the
blame. It was after all a British leader (in American eyes *the* British
leader), Winston Churchill, who in 1946 gave the first resounding
expression to the ideal of European unity in his Zurich speech
advocating a "kind of United States of Europe". Two years later it
was a British Foreign Secretary, Ernest Bevin, who announced his
belief that the time was "ripe for a consolidation of Western
Europe" and talked about "Western Union". No doubt, as events
showed, the British Government attached its own qualified significance to this term, but they ought to have known that read on the
other side of the Atlantic the phrase could bear only two meanings;
it was either the name of a private company engaged in the tele-
graph business or it stood for a federal government on an American
model. How little the United Kingdom meant the latter was
quickly shown by the Labour Party's refusal to send any representative to the "Congress of Europe" launched in 1948 as the fore-
runner of the Council of Europe. This was underlined by the Bevin
sneer in the House of Commons: "I amalgamated a lot of unions
into one union but the first thing I looked at was the assets." When
in 1950 the Schuman plan was proposed the British refusal to co-
operate was given a needlessly arrogant and doctrinaire twist by

the coincidental publication of the Labour Executive's pamphlet on "European Unity"; this manifesto of British isolationism, though not a Government statement, was sufficiently close to one to necessitate the British ambassador in Washington proffering an official apologia to the Senate Foreign Relations Committee. Finally the hopes raised by Conservative Party spokesmen when in opposition were rudely dashed when Churchill came to power in 1951 and revealed himself on this issue as no more co-operative in practice (and not much more mollifying in manner) than his Labour predecessors. Small wonder that when the European idea revived in the later fifties and was accorded a much more serious consideration in Britain the United States remained sceptical of Britain doing anything much of her own volition and consequently took it upon herself again to be a persistent gadfly in the cause.

In Britain the depth and intensity of American commitment to this cause were often not appreciated or, when felt, not understood. Facile explanations about the United States being a federation and so regarding federalism as the only wear do less than justice to the impulses behind the American attitude. The Americans were not hawking a nostrum of political science but projecting their whole national experience—indeed their *raison d'être* as a nation. America *is* a united Europe, a society and culture, as well as a government, within which all the peoples of Europe (and some others as well) have found it possible to live and let live. To recommend this achievement of the New World for the emulation of the Old was therefore not a disinterested act of benevolence or a gratuitous piece of impertinence, according to taste, but a preachment which America could no more forego than she could abandon the reason for her own being or dissolve the glue of her own nationhood. If this *causa causans* had been understood then many of the anomalies of American support for European union would have been seen to be illusory.

Within this consistent American movement of support for European integration three rough phases can be distinguished. The first is the period of active pressure on Western Europe and particularly on Britain, as the most sluggish member of the side. This is linked to America's role in the creation of the American-European institutions such as N.A.T.O. and O.E.E.C. on which Europe depended. The second phase, beginning with the establishment of the European Coal and Steel Community and synchronizing[2] roughly with the change-over from Truman to Eisenhower, sees an abatement of American pressure on the United Kingdom to go into Europe and a certain willingness to accept the unification of the Six as a substitute for anything more comprehensive. The third phase begins with the effective establishment of the Common Market and is dominated by a complex blend of American reactions—support for the new venture combined with a new concern about its implications for American economic and diplomatic interests.

In the first phase the disposition in the United States was strong to demand some European integration as a return for American aid, the demand being justified on the grounds that so long as the national economies of Europe remained unintegrated they would continue to be non-viable and so become recurrent charges on the American tax-payer. It was in these terms that the preamble to the European Co-operation Act (E.C.A.) in June, 1948, formulated American intentions and expectations:

"Mindful of the advantages which the United States has enjoyed through the existence of a large domestic market with no internal barriers to trade or to the free movement of persons, and believing that similar advantages can accrue to the countries of Europe, it is declared to be the policy of the people of the United States to encourage these countries through their joint organization to exert sustained common efforts to achieve speedily that economic co-operation in Europe which is essential for lasting peace and prosperity."

The following year's Act repeated these sentiments and added: "It is further declared to be the policy of the people of the United States to encourage the unification of Europe." When Mutual Security replaced Marshall Aid the same objectives of "economic unification and political federation" were avowed in the authorizing legislation. And the Republican opposition was every bit as vocal in these sentiments as the Democratic administration. It was Mr. Dewey campaigning for the Presidency who announced in Salt Lake City on 30 September, 1948: "We shall use [the programme of aid to Europe] as the means for pushing, prodding and encouraging the nations of Western Europe towards the goal of European union."

Wisely, for all the fervour of their advocacy, American integrationists stopped short of actually requiring from any European state any surrender of powers to a supra-national organization. In resisting specific movements in this direction the British were undoubtedly foremost and they shaped the institutions of the Marshall Plan, such as the weak O.E.E.C. secretariat, with a determination to prevent any such development. Within these limits, however, the British were at least as active as other recipient states in promoting co-operation amongst the European economies. As one close American observer of O.E.E.C. later wrote, the British "provided first-class personnel and a quality of diplomatic leadership which played a major role in developing common European attitudes towards the recovery problems and a willingness to subordinate particular interests to the wider needs".[1] In the labours of E.P.U. in making multilateral payments possible and in the application of its Code of Trade Liberalization the British were as active as anyone—and, it may fairly be claimed, as co-operative.

As the European Recovery Programme realized its initial objective of salvaging Western European economies and liberalizing Western European trade, and as the Korean War stimulated the demand for German rearmament, the second phase of American policy towards European unity began to develop. The emphasis switched from the economic to the military and it was the future of the European Defence Community which most exercised Washington—and indeed London. On the economic front there was, if not a greater agreement with the British position, at least a readier acceptance of it, partly no doubt because the continental powers were now going ahead on their own; American policy stimulated and assisted the Europeanists on the continent rather than any longer goading the reluctant British into joining an operation for which they felt no enthusiasm. The assistance took sometimes a direct form, like the 1954 loan of $100 million to E.C.S.C. or the 1958 credit of $135 million to Euratom, together with the 20-years supply of enriched uranium fuel and American participation in a $100 million joint research and development programme. The stimulation was sometimes indirect and unintentional; thus paradoxically the experience of Suez, driving home the impotence of France and the insufficiency of Europe's fuel resources, stimulated the "Third Force" advocates of European union and the believers in Euratom as a short cut to plentiful supplies of fuel and power.

For Britain these were years when neither type of inducement

[1] Lincoln Gordon on O.E.E.C., in *International Organisation*, 1956, p. 3.

counted for much. Returning prosperity, despite recurrent weaknesses in the balance of payments, encouraged the belief that there was no need, economically, to go into Europe. Consequently when all other considerations pointed in the direction of cultivating a bilateral relationship with the U.S.A., the disposition was general, in economic as in military policy, to adopt towards Europe a kind of British variant of the American line—i.e. to support European unification from *outside*, to offer all aid short of coming in. Even during the year of estrangement, 1956, the Anglo-French alliance on the Middle East had no counterpart on the European front, and from the collapse of the Suez venture, as we have seen, a very different moral was drawn in London from that which gained acceptance in Paris.

Thus down to the ratification of the Rome Treaties by France and Germany in July, 1957, Britain did not feel that the progressive consolidation of the Six constituted a serious problem for her, nor that the admitted difference of views between London and Washington over Britain's role in Europe was anything more than an amicable agreement to differ. The Americans had dropped their forcing policy; the implications of the Six had yet to emerge. The painful British awakening came first with the dawning realization of what the European Economic Community (E.E.C.) could mean to her. Her first response took the form of exploring the idea of a European free trade area, co-extensive with O.E.E.C., an abortive enterprise in which she may have been encouraged (whether advisedly or no) by the expression of occasional American anxieties about E.E.C.'s possible discrimination against non-members. However, as 1958 went on, French hostility to the free trade area hardened without any corresponding rise in American anxieties about the Community. Rather the reverse. In the O.E.E.C. meetings of December, 1958, when Sir David Eccles for Britain and M. Couve de Murville for France became deadlocked in their violent disagreement over the virtues of their respective "Area" and "Community", it was taken as an omen that the American observer at the session was curiously silent when asked for the views of the United States. The explanation was not far to seek, but it was political more than economic. In American eyes a rarely favourable juncture had arrived in the affairs of continental Europe. France, under De Gaulle, had a government that could govern; Germany still had in Adenauer a ruler unshakeably committed to the West.

146

But for how long? He was old and he did not lack enemies. In the plans for the Community these two pillars of anti-Communism had found an accord which the Americans desperately wished to make permanent, by binding France and Germany in the institutions, initially economic but finally political, of the Six. Only so, it was felt, in face of Russian pressure, could Western Germany resist the attractions of neutralism with its inviting rider of possible reunification. By comparison, the British were somewhat less committed to the idea of a Western Germany permanently and militarily bound to the West. In 1958–60 they were prepared, at least in return for a real settlement with Russia, to envisage an atom-free zone in Central Europe on Rapacki lines or at least a negotiated *status quo*. For such a policy a Franco-German fusion was a good deal less than necessary.

When Mr. Macmillan visited Washington in March, 1959, to lay plans for an agreed approach to "summit" talks with Mr. Khrushchev there was an obvious connexion between his desire that the West should retain the maximum freedom of negotiation over Germany and his concern lest the U.S.A. should pledge herself to the Six. On the German question in relation to summit talks a working (or perhaps one should say a paper) agreement was reached but on the subject of the economic split in Europe the Americans remained unpersuaded.

After what happened at the Eccles-de Murville encounter, and against the known background of American attitudes to European unity, this should have occasioned no surprise. The fact was that a new and more positive phase of American policy was under way. Significantly, it was associated with, and indeed largely directed by Mr. Dillon, who in 1957 joined the State Department as Deputy Under-Secretary of State for Economic Affairs. A known Francophile and intimate of M. Jean Monnet, Mr. Dillon was an appropriate mouthpiece for a policy which backed the "Europeanists". But he was more than a mouthpiece. Mr. Dillon belonged, as conspicuously as anyone in the late fifties, to that American "Establishment" of internationally-minded lawyers-cum-Wall Street bankers whose association with foreign policy-making has been continuous in Washington, irrespective of administrations, ever since Roosevelt's presidency in the mid-thirties. In the last years of the Eisenhower régime, as Dulles's powers failed, Mr. Dillon became a key figure in the shaping of American economic policy.

The United States indeed had its own worries about the Common Market, but they were rooted in something quite different, and indeed quite novel, in an economic development which Europeans found hard to appreciate—the deterioration in America's balance of payments. The deterioration first began to attract attention in 1958 when the American annual deficit rose to $3·4 billion from a "normal" figure of about $1½ billion. For 1959 the figure was $4 billion. That there should be a United States "dollar problem" within ten years of the launching of the Marshall Plan was something which to Britain and indeed to all European ears was scarcely credible. In fact it was largely a consequence of the success which had attended American efforts to promote European recovery. When at Christmas, 1958, the pound and other principal European currencies were made externally convertible the result was to promote a movement of capital from the once overwhelmingly attractive dollar area to the centres of high interest rates in Europe. Most of this was no doubt "hot money" rather than long-term investment, but coming at a time of lowered vitality in the American economy it was naturally a matter of concern in Washington. In particular it promoted an American demand that the U.S.A.'s European allies should take a larger share of the burdens of economic aid to the underdeveloped countries and the cost of the common defence, and also that they should not discriminate against American exports. It was principally in this last connexion that the Common Market aroused American apprehensions. This however did not mean, as was all too readily assumed in Britain, that the American stance on this issue was becoming identical with the British. Far from it.

Having failed to persuade the Six to float their Common Market in a larger European free trade area, the British proceeded in 1959 to create out of the seven excluded O.E.E.C. members a Free Trade Association of their own. This was intended to be a protective and bargaining association which would, by the threats of reprisals, persuade the Community to maintain liberal trade relations with the Seven. Natural though such a counter-alliance might be for its members, it was too much to expect that it should enjoy American backing. In so far as it weakened the Six it would frustrate the political hopes which, as we have seen, the Americans attached to the Community. In so far as its trade bargaining was successful the net result might easily be an agreement between the two blocs to practise a joint discrimination against third parties, of which the U.S.A. would be the main victim. Finally a protracted duel between the Six and the Seven would impede the realization of the U.S.A.'s other urgent objective, of securing European assistance with overseas aid and defence costs; instead of uniting in the common tasks of the alliance, Europe would split into two camps with ill-feeling (as became very apparent by the end of 1959) rising daily between the two sets of rivals. Thus though the United States and Britain had an interest in resolving the conflict it was not an identical interest.

When therefore both Six and Seven accepted in December, 1959, the American proposal of a Paris meeting at which they would talk to each other (and to the United States) for the first time since December, 1958, it was with considerably different expectations and objectives that Britain and the United States approached the conference table. From the British point of view the meetings were only semi-satisfactory. The Americans gave a low priority to the healing of the rift between Six and Seven and on this no tangible progress was made, beyond the setting up of a twenty-nation group (the old O.E.E.C. membership but not under O.E.E.C. auspices) to keep communications open. Instead the Americans insistently pressed for action on the aid front and launched the idea of a successor body to O.E.E.C. which should co-ordinate (and increase) the aid programmes of member states and which would have the U.S.A. as a principal participant. As negotiations went on throughout the spring and summer, argument developed on the powers of this successor body, the O.E.C.D. (Organization for Economic Co-operation and Development). The smaller European states, assisted by Britain, pressed for the inclusion, amongst its objectives, not only of aid and economic growth, but also of trade expansion. At the end of July the U.S.A. gave in on this point, on the clear understanding that she could not be bound, in the tariff field, by any collective decision of the Organization, and on 14 December, 1960, the convention was signed at Paris establishing O.E.C.D. to come into effect in 1961 when the requisite number of members ratified the agreement.

Meanwhile, however, the conflict of Six and Seven had grown sharper and given rise to further asperities between London and Washington. When the Six proposed in March, 1960, to accelerate their union by enforcing their common external tariff on 1 July instead of the original date of 1 January, 1962, the Seven received this as a severe jolt to their hopes of a negotiated settlement. It was obvious that the Six were deliberately hurrying to put themselves in a position where no pressure from the Seven could undo their partnership. Worse still, this move appeared to enjoy American blessing. What other interpretation could be put on the phrase in the communiqué issued at the end of the Eisenhower-Adenauer meeting, on 14 March, which spoke of the proposal as "a major contribution to a general lowering of world trade barriers"? When later in the month Mr. Macmillan visited Washington in his turn, ostensibly to resolve differences over nuclear tests and disarmament in preparation for the "summit" meeting in May, this issue was almost as much on his mind as the problems of east and west. At this visit, as in 1959, an agreement, somewhat more procedural than substantive, was reached on east-west issues, but there was no meeting of minds over the Common Market issue. Indeed so complacent an indifference to the British point of view did Mr. Macmillan encounter that he apparently felt it necessary to shock his American hosts with a vehement expression of his views on the approaching rift in Europe. He was subsequently reported (in a Washington "leak" whose authenticity was not wholly denied by British officials) as reminding Mr. Dillon that once before, in Napoleon's day, Britain had frustrated French attempts at establishing a hegemony in Europe.

The Six meanwhile had taken the precaution, in planning their acceleration, of offering a "sweetener" to the United States in the form of a 20 per cent cut in their common tariff for any other states who might offer a *quid pro quo*. The United States administration liked this as a talking-point with Congress in their campaign for freer trade and were similarly assisted a couple of months later, in June, when the Six offered a comparable concession to the only openly hostile American pressure group, the farmers, by announcing the abandonment of any direct quantitative restrictions against grain imports, as well as certain tariff reductions for American tobacco.

Thus 1960 continued with no abatement of American support for the Six and no sign of American willingness to act as broker between them and the Seven. Increasingly, as the presidential election approached and President Eisenhower's own mandate ran out, it became impossible to hope for any change of direction or new impetus from Washington. Fortunately for Britain, however, some change was occurring on the continent. Though the impulse for the Common Market did not wane, the process and the goals of unification were being modified under the nationalistic instincts of General de Gaulle. His conception of *L'Europe des Patries* produced a shift in the decision-making of the Six away from the federalists at Brussels to the individual governments in their sovereignty-conscious capitals. This implied a considerably more limited political objective for the Common Market and one much more acceptable to the British. At the same time as this change occurred in Paris, a ferment was working in Bonn. Here anxiety was developing not so much over a supra-nationalist Six but over the hyper-nationalist One, to wit de Gaulle. The relentless refusal of the French President to co-operate in the political and military processes of N.A.T.O. except on his own terms was causing not only irritation but also (especially since the collapse of the "summit" in May) a real anxiety about its effect on the Atlantic alliance. In meetings held at the end of July and the beginning of August this came to a head. Dr. Adenauer, it would seem, was disappointed at Rambouillet that he could not move General de Gaulle by considerations of this kind. Mr. Macmillan coming to Bonn soon afterwards found the Chancellor in consequence especially receptive to his contention that French leadership was taking Western Europe out of the Atlantic alliance into a "Third Force" isolation and that to stop this the Germans must throw a bridge by which the Europes of the Six and the Seven could reunite in an Atlantic alliance under American leadership. Whatever exactly was said in these meetings a new mood seems to have developed; the British thought more kindly of a Common Market which would not aim at a precipitate federalism and the Germans were now positively in favour of healing the split. Both changes of heart seem to have come without any shadow or hint of encouragement from Washington, but both reflected a dominating awareness of Western Europe's need of America.

The year ended with a significant demonstration of America's need of Europe. The continuing weakness in the American balance of payments led by the autumn to a further sharp drain on the U.S.A.'s gold reserves. In a series of measures reminiscent of British policy in 1947 or 1951 President Eisenhower directed all federal agencies to cut down their spending abroad, required a stricter "Buy American" policy for foreign aid funds and ordered a reduction of 200,000 in the number of service dependents living abroad. At the same time Mr. Anderson, the Secretary of the Treasury, and Mr. Dillon visited Bonn to press for a $600 million contribution towards the cost of maintaining American troops on German soil. The ill-timed and tactless proposal provoked a jarring refusal and an unacceptable set of counter-proposals. Only London, where the Bank of England forced gold prices down by using, in part, gold bought from the official United States reserves, was able to give immediate aid to the giant of the Atlantic alliance.

Thus already by the end of 1960 a variety of factors was making for a revision of Britain's position on the question of "going into Europe". The switch from a rather run-down Eisenhower presidency to a brisk and enterprising Kennedy administration did not alter any of the elements entering into the triangular relationship between Britain, the United States and the Common Market, but it considerably accelerated their operation. Any Kennedy expectations that French irritation at "the Anglo-American directorate" could be easily eliminated, as for example by the Presidential state visit to Paris in June, foundered on the irrefrangible rock of de Gaulle's "one-outmanship". Over N.A.T.O., over Berlin, over the United Nations, over nuclear weapons, there was little or no effective Franco-American *rapprochement*. But this in no way diminished the American conviction of the political desirability of an economically united Europe; indeed it intensified it, on the principle that the only abrasive which might reduce French spinosity would be her incorporation in a larger whole. The continuing American balance of payments problem pointed in the same direction; only an economically integrated Europe, it increasingly seemed, could give the United States effective assistance in the reallocation of the burdens of common defence and overseas aid. Finally, the new fillip which Kennedy dynamism was willing to give to the thirty-year-old American drive for freer trade required as an absolute *sine qua non* a comparable dynamism in the form of European integration.

From the British point of view, equally, the pressures that had been forming in 1960 intensified themselves in 1961. The high price of exclusion from a closely integrated Six came to seem ever more costly. The scope for possible leadership in a new Europe began to seem more attractive. American pressures towards integration did not abate. What was more, the willingness of the Kennedy administration really to carry forward the earlier hints of a liberal trading policy over the whole Atlantic area went far to remove the deepest of British fears, that involvement in Europe would mean detachment from the U.S.A. If the United States was really prepared to lower her own tariffs and to press for a low external tariff in the Common Market then a new way seemed open by which Britain could reconcile her interests throughout the Commonwealth, across the Atlantic and across the Channel.

Though it suited the British Government to give the impression that it found a new attitude in Washington towards the problems of British entry into the Common Market (cf. much British press comment after Mr. Macmillan's Washington visit in April, 1961), the real difference lay elsewhere. It manifested itself in the presence of some new faces at the top,[1] in a new approach, at once more pragmatic and more aware of Britain's peculiar problems, and above all in a greater sense of urgency. When the long-accumulating pressure finally tipped the scales and Her Majesty's Government made their historic decision on 31 July, 1961, to apply for admission to the Community, this was nowhere received with more gratification than in the United States. "We welcome," said President Kennedy, "the prospect of Britain's participation in the institutions of the Treaty of Rome and in the economic growth that is the achievement and promise of the Common Market."

---

[1] Though not all of these were new, e.g. Mr. Dillon.

II

THE BRITISH ECONOMY AND THE
UNITED STATES

EVEN before the war the British economy had more links with the American than with any other in the world, the Commonwealth countries alone excepted. American booms or slumps, the raising or lowering of American tariffs, had a peculiar significance for Britain by virtue of the exceptionally intimate trading relationships of the two countries. Even in 1938, when the total value of world trade had fallen to sixty-eight per cent of what it had been ten years earlier and when the development of Imperial Preference had cut into the traditional patterns of Anglo-American trading—even then the United Kingdom and the United States between them were directly responsible for about one quarter of the world's trade, while "the Anglo-American group" (i.e. the British Commonwealth and both Americas) accounted for virtually half.[1] In direct trading 12·8 per cent of all United Kingdom exports came from the United States (only the Dominions supplied more) and 6 per cent of all American imports came from Britain (only Canada and Japan sent more). If 6 per cent seems a modest figure (it represented only 5·4 per cent of British exports) the explanation lay, of course, in the pattern of indirect, multilateral trading which, for example, sales of Malayan tin and rubber to the U.S.A. helped to make up the difference. The British-American trading relationship was indeed a crucial part of a world-wide system to whose functioning both London and New York were indispensable.

Even so, there was an imbalance in the relationship in 1938 and had been for some years. Even when the trading with third parties was added in, Britain's trading accounts did not balance. Between 1936 and 1938 the excess of Britain's merchandise imports over her exports averaged £388 million a year, a sum which invisible exports such as shipping, banking, insurance services, etc., did not suffice to make up. Britain was living off her overseas investments

[1] *The Network of World Trade* (League of Nations, 1942), p. 69.

—and off the capital, as well as the interest. In terms which his successors were frequently to echo the President of the Board of Trade warned the House of Commons that the early months of 1938 had shown a worsening in the balance of payments position with the United States so pronounced as to be "disquieting".

In other words Imperial Preference had not solved the problems of Britain as a trading nation. She still needed imports which only the U.S.A. could supply. She still had to find some way of paying for them. The negotiation in 1938 of the Anglo-American Trade Agreement was a recognition of this. Britain and America reduced their tariffs on imports from each other and, of course, thereby gave most-favoured nation treatment to other traders too. Hesitant and reluctant though it was, the Agreement represented a move away from Ottawa, a response to Mr. Cordell Hull's belief in a liberal world of multilateral trade. Even if there had been no war, Britain was thus committed to responding to the magnetic pull of American commercial policy. When war did break out, what had been a persuasive attraction became an urgent compulsion.

The war produced a swift and progressive British dependence on North America for all essential supplies, with Lend Lease taking the place of normal methods of payment. Unfortunately much of the endemic weakness in the British position came to be mistakenly attributed to the abnormal strains of war, with the result that the country entered the peace without a full, instinctive comprehension of the economic task before it. The United States itself was prone to a comparable error, as was demonstrated by the various miscalculations embodied in the Anglo-American Financial Agreements of 1946.

In consequence weaknesses in the British position which might have been accurately predicted by any dispassionate student of pre-war economic trends broke upon the publics of each country as a disconcerting series of "crises" in the fifteen years after the end of the war. The British balance of payments looked like the temperature chart of a patient with undulant fever, one attack developing as its predecessor died away. The British Government found itself repeatedly obliged to turn to America for aid or to adopt successive short-term policies at odds with its long-term commitments to the United States. Britain's post-war impoverishment was relieved by the American and Canadian loans only to be succeeded by the convertibility crisis of 1947 and the ensuing devaluation of the pound. The strains produced by the Korean war and the American "recession" of 1950 led to the tightening controls of Mr. Attlee's last year in 1951. In 1955 Mr. Butler as Chancellor of the Exchequer had to repeat the medicine, raising the bank rate by $1\frac{1}{2}$ per cent to $4\frac{1}{2}$ per cent (the highest rate since 1932), imposing a credit squeeze in the summer and bringing in a supplementary budget in the autumn. The Suez fiasco of 1956 produced an immediate run on the pound and led in 1957 to the invocation of the payments waiver provided for in the Anglo-American Financial Agreements and the raising of a $500 million line of credit from the Export-Import Bank, Even though 1958 ended with *de jure* convertibility restored for current transactions and 1959 saw a real improvement in Britain's basic economic position, which permitted the removal of licensing requirements over virtually the whole field of imports, even then all was not well. The old weakness redeveloped in 1960 leading to another 7 per cent peak in the Bank rate in 1961. 1961–2 also saw the profits and wages "pause", and a persistently inadequate level of gold and dollar reserves. However much Britain's difficulties might be the result of efforts in a common cause, it was embarrassing to be seeking recurrent American aid. It was even more embarrassing when, as after Suez, they were largely the result of over-exertion in a far from common cause.

Embarrassment apart, the weakness of Britain's reserves on more than one occasion prevented her playing a full part in the various common enterprises to which the two countries were committed. We have seen how American hopes for a swift post-war return to multilateral trading conditions rested upon an exaggerated estimate of the tempo of British recovery. Here at least the British were not to blame; their warning notes were so loud and clear as to be written off as alarmist. But the British Government itself was slow to recognize the restraints imposed by its balance of payments position. Americans could fairly complain of the suddenness of the Treasury's awakening which led to the withdrawal from Greece and Turkey. Both in Korea itself and in the European rearmament programme which was its corollary British efforts were limited by restricted overseas resources. In the launching of any common economic venture, from the U.N. Expanded Programme of Technical Assistance to the salvaging of India's Five-Year Plans, the British share has had to be so severely limited as to leave her too little power of initiation or, comparatively speaking, of control. Finally, in enterprises where the British interest was predominant, such as the salvaging of the British oil investment in Mossadeq's Persia, Britain's economic stringency left her so little scope for movement that she was really dependent on American aid for the achievement of a satisfactory solution. When, as over Suez, this was denied, the result was failure.

The harmful consequences of this weakness in the British balance of payments would have been much greater if Britain had not secured official American acceptance (at least after 1947) of the necessity for protective discriminatory measures, at least in the short run. Without an apparatus of controls, involving a rigid elimination of all non-essential dollar purchases, Britain's payments position would have been enormously, impossibly worse. But however ready Washington officials might be to accept the need for this,[1] Congressmen who voted aid funds and were highly susceptible to constituency pressures of every kind were seldom so sympathetic. They showed a marked reluctance to recognize that the quickest way to become independent of American aid was to buy as little from the dollar area as possible. It was one thing to accept this as an intellectual proposition; another thing to make it palatable to American taxpayers who made their living out of goods they hoped to sell to overseas customers, the British included. It was thus a welcome day in 1959 when, in recognition of the first British trade surplus with the United States in a hundred years, import controls were removed from all but a very small range of dollar goods. The quantitative rise in imports was not enormous (about £50 million in 1960) but it had something of the same kind of token significance as the 1957 easement of the currency restrictions on travel to dollar areas. The dollar curtain which, for all the intimacies of officialdom, had hung between the New World and the British private citizen as consumer or traveller ever since 1939 was at last beginning to disappear. The eventual consequences of a restoration of real freedom of movement for goods and persons in

[1] Sometimes they were not very ready, either because they had a psychology of boldness such as only the rich can afford or because they were doctrinaire liberals of a highly conservative kind, or because like all American officials they had to serve two masters, Congress as well as the President.

both directions across the North Atlantic might well be as significant for Britain in the sixties as any official pact between London
and Washington.

The quotas were removed but the tariffs remained. The history
of British-American tariff squabbles is a long and edifying one, the
details of which, even since 1938, defy brief analysis. But a few
salient features stand out. Thanks mainly to the action taken by
successive American Presidents under successive Trade Agreements
Acts, from Roosevelt in 1934 to Mr. Kennedy, who secured a
notable expansion of such authority in 1962, the American tariff
against British imports has fallen by sometimes between 50 and 75
per cent overall, though any single figure necessarily conceals wide
individual variations for certain categories of goods. The British
tariff against American goods on the other hand remains very little
changed and provides British producers with a considerably more
effective protection than their American opposite numbers enjoy.
This has not been fully appreciated in Britain or in the United
States, partly because the operative restrictions on trade have been
those imposed by quota and currency regulations, but also because
of the different significance that transatlantic trade has had for the
two economies.

For Britain, trade with North America and particularly with the
United States has been absolutely crucial. Even at the height of
Imperial Preference, even at the worst periods of dollar shortage,
Britain has been heavily dependent upon imports from the U.S.A.
because she alone could provide items that were essential to
Britain; consequently, until most of the world's major currencies
became convertible again, the imperative of the British mercantile
economy has been the provision of exports to pay for them. For the
United States on the other hand foreign trade in general, including
trade to Britain, however desirable and even for certain products
(e.g. tobacco) essential, has not been the vital core of the country's
economic life. Though self-sufficiency has never been practicable in
terms of the economic and other goals the United States has chosen
to set herself, such as a high standard of living, free enterprise and
heavy political commitments overseas, the natural resources of the
country are basically adequate for the support of its population in a
way that those of the United Kingdom have not been for over three
hundred years. When therefore the American legislator and official
turn their attention to trade it is either in terms of protecting some

particular and generally local interest or in terms of furthering some quasi-political objective—cf. the almost Cobdenite philosophy behind the Trade Agreements Acts. For the British parliament and government, however, once the *laissez-faire* tradition had been broken down[1] the furtherance of Britain's trade came near to having an absolute priority as a *sine qua non* on which all else in the nation's life depended.

Thus the British exporter's eye has always been quick to mark (and the British journalist to headline) the least American threat to British products, while the American Congressman (and the American leader-writer) have been much more sensitive to a British trading transaction which violated a political prejudice (e.g. trade with the Communist bloc) than to British tariff levels in general.

In consequence British trade policy as far as the United States is concerned has very often appeared to consist of a series of protests against malpractices which Americans regard as minor, the wool tariff quota or the "escape clause" tariff on bicycles, and of justifications for peccancies which the Americans regard as major, such as the sale of raw rubber to the U.S.S.R. or Vickers Viscounts to China. The British argument in each case has been essentially the same; in the former case, that restrictions which are minor in relation to the gigantic American economy may be major in the effect they have on Britain's balance of payments; in the latter case, that Britain cannot afford the luxury of foregoing trade with political opponents save where it is conclusively demonstrated that its effect would be to assist them in indubitably inimical enterprises. The success which each category of arguments has won in the United States has varied according to the domestic political situation and the rise or fall in East-West temperatures. British attitudes over each type of dispute are not likely to change in a foreseeable future, rooted as they are in the persistent facts of her economic life, but it is possible that the somewhat disproportionate significance that such issues have assumed in Anglo-American policy may decline. The development of the European Common Market and the change in the American balance of payments are already pointers to a likely American counter-offensive aimed at making sizeable breaches in all European tariff walls and in expanding North Atlantic trade all round. At the same time post-Dulles policy in the United States has come to favour a more pragmatic approach to problems of East-

[1] And indeed before it was established.

West relations and so (Cuba apart) is less likely to treat all forms of trade with Communist countries as a traffic with the mammon of unrighteousness.

The issues mentioned above do not exhaust the range of Anglo-American commercial controversies which have their roots in the persistent American temptation to use the great power of the American Government to assist special interests or sectors of the American economy and in the hypersensitiveness of the United Kingdom to anything which interferes with her world-wide trading interests. Thus a long-standing rivalry in shipping has provided in its modest way some of the most acrimonious Anglo-American exchanges of the post-war period, with each side damning the sins it had no mind to. Britain, the possessor of a great and indispensable merchant marine, privately built,[1] owned and operated, was content to rely on the advantages of skill, world-wide bases and connexions and low operating costs (at least as compared with North America), plus the bargaining advantages that naturally accrued to her as a great bulk importer. For the American economy in peacetime its mercantile marine was much less important, and, by reason of high costs, much more expensive to build and maintain; yet for obvious reasons it could not be allowed to collapse before the play of purely economic forces. In full knowledge of this strategic indispensability the American shipping interests could always secure generous assistance from Congress. The building and operating subsidies which they enjoyed were, in British eyes, "unfair" and objectionable enough, but when in 1954 the Cargo Preference Act was passed a new kind of mercantilism appeared on the American statute book. Britain, along with other seafaring recipients, had reluctantly accepted the principles written into Marshall Aid, Mutual Security legislation and the like that fifty per cent of the cargoes involved should be carried in American bottoms; they were American "gifts" and had to be accepted on American terms. But the Cargo Preference Act went a considerable step farther; it extended the principle to cargoes even indirectly financed with government funds and excluded, for purposes of calculating the fifty per cent, cargoes carried in government-owned ships. To Britain the Act was doubly objectionable; in itself and as an incentive to other countries to adopt similar discriminating legislation. The issue acquired a double, and

[1] Except for the government assistance supplied to Cunard for the construction of the "Queen" liners.

sharper edge in 1959 with talk of America's need to conserve dollars in the interest of her balance of payments and at the same time to enlist European countries in a common policy of aid to the "underdevelopeds". Could she have it both ways? In June, 1959, Britain made joint representations with eight other European countries; then and in 1960 British Ministers of Transport made strong, even indignant, protests in Washington. They were unavailing. The American shipowners indeed were stimulated to stronger measures. They contended that Britain was restricting competition by the device of the shipping conference, the British-inspired institutions which regulate services and freights on all the main shipping lines across the world. Invoking the sacred principles of anti-trust law, Congress in 1961 authorized the President to "disallow" freight rates negotiated by such a procedure. And so the battle went on.

In general, where American foreign aid is concerned, considering the pressures playing on Congress and the opportunities afforded by the gigantic and diverse aid programmes, the British manufacturer and exporter has had less reason to complain of American self-favouritism in this field than he might reasonably have expected. Yet inevitably there is a dual aspect to all American activity of this kind and the benefit it creates for American producers and exporters are bound to be most acutely felt by the country which of all others has the longest tradition of trade competition with the U.S.A. and stands to lose most by being ousted from any of its old markets. The United States cannot indulge in the benevolent exercise of establishing an International Atomic Energy Agency without at the same time creating certain predispositions in favour of reliance on American-produced equipment. She cannot participate in the salvaging of the Indian Five-Year Plans, a high priority of British Commonwealth policy, without invading a long-cherished domain of British commerce. There must consequently always be for Britain a double reaction to all American ventures in the international economic field; she welcomes them as the indispensable blood transfusion without which successive embolisms would bring the economic circulation of the free world to a paralytic standstill; at the same time she has to scrutinize every point where the life-giving American fluid is applied to see that it does not swamp an established British connexion or deny Britain a fair competitive share of the opportunities created.

Thus Britain has always been hyper-sensitive to any American

aid programme which obliged recipients to spend their dollars on
American goods. Not only is any such tied aid objectionable in
itself but when indulged in by the U.S.A. it has the added fault of
constituting a bad example which others of Britain's trading competitors, such as Germany, are only too ready to emulate. Unfortunately, with the emerging weakness of America's balance of payments the temptation to resort to this protective device has increased
and is likely to persist. There is of course a certain contradiction
between American advocacy of increased aid and her adoption of a
device which virtually guarantees a cut in the real value of all such
aid.[1] Nonetheless, logic has been more than once over-borne by
sectional pressures and doubtless will be again.

In another context a comparable connexion between American
aid and Anglo-American economic rivalry may be observed.
Within N.A.T.O. a keen competition persists between Britain and
the U.S.A. for the provision of agreed weapons to other partners
in the alliance, conspicuously Germany. When the West Germans
began rearming it was the United States which provided free,
under Mutual Aid, their initial equipment. The habits thereby
established were hard to break and American sales pressure, responding to America's own balance of payments needs, took up
where American gifts left off. At the distasteful point at which
politics, economics and rearmament meet, the Americans enjoy an
obvious advantage from their preponderant role in the alliance. It
is consequently hardly surprising that it was May, 1961, before the
first substantial German armaments order was placed in London.

Of quite another order is the question of American investment
in Britain. Here the Government has had to face a problem created
largely by its own need to save dollars and so to discriminate against
dollar goods. To overcome the obstacles thus placed in the path of
their exports an increasing number of American firms have established branches in Britain. Exact figures of the total investment
involved are hard to come by, since no official statistics appear to be
kept in Whitehall, but the total of United States investment in the
United Kingdom has risen from approximately $450 million in
1938 to $3,194 million at the end of 1960. Although spread over

[1] Because, of course, manufacturers supplying to such a protected
market feel free to raise their prices without any worries about consumer resistance. The average effect on American aid, it has been
calculated, is to cut the real value by 25 per cent.

hundreds of firms, this American investment has been mainly concentrated in the oil, motor car, chemical and aluminium industries. In an economy for whose oversight the state assumes so much greater responsibility than before the war, the British Government has necessarily had to concern itself with this phenomenon. In general it has been sympathetic to such investment, mainly for its direct dollar benefits but also, in certain cases, for the indirect gains accruing from the introduction of American productive techniques or the results of American research. But it also tests each application in the light of a set of principles which the Dollar Exports Council has defined as follows :

"It is necessary that the project should be of sufficient benefit to the British economy to justify such dollar expenditure [on transfer of dividends or possible repatriation of capital] either because it will earn or save hard currency, or because it is a valuable addition to the country's industrial efficiency. . . . New schemes [should] not involve unreasonable additional dollar outgoings for royalties, extra raw materials or components, payments to foreign technicians and similar charges."

In other words American investment has been welcomed provided it meets all the requirements imposed by the weakness of Britain's balance of payments. Even so, should it be welcomed? The question has been pressed whenever a sizeable slice of any British industry has in consequence come under American control, as in 1960 when Ford of Detroit purchased the minority shareholding of Ford of Dagenham. It is the familiar menace, in a slightly different form, of the American colossus crushing the British economy by sheer size and weight. But notable though the post-war rise in American investment has been there is no evidence that it has seriously or banefully affected the working of British industry. Rather, indeed, the reverse.[1] Moreover, notable though one or two recent moves have been, the changes in the two countries' balance of payments and the regulations thus induced, together with the rising attraction for American capital of the Common Market, strongly suggest that the peak point of American investment in the United Kingdom has

[1] For a summary of arguments pro and con see John H. Dunning, *American Investment in British Manufacturing Industry* (London, Fair Lawn—New Jersey, 1958).

by now been passed. In any case the whole movement cannot be viewed in isolation. It is partly a particular aspect of that "mixing up" of the two countries' affairs which, if welcome in other fields, cannot be eliminated from this. More than this, it is also one expression of that multilateralism to which in respect of all other economic activities Britain is deeply committed. Finally, were Britain to oppose this manifestation of American enterprise her position would be particularly hard to maintain, since British investment in the United States is one of the oldest and most respectable strands in Anglo-American relations. Although many British holdings had to be liquidated in the early days of the war for the purchase of essential requirements, more than $3,750 million's worth of American shares are now in the hands of either the British Government or private investors. In April, 1959, the Chancellor of the Exchequer announced that, taking Canada and the U.S.A. together, British investment in North America probably fully matched American investment in Britain.

Such conflicts of interest, real or imagined, as have been outlined above have provided the focus for most of the discussion and controversy in Britain about economic relations with the United States since the war. This is perhaps natural, but it is nonetheless unfortunate. It has the result of giving an exaggeratedly nationalist and political twist to what are essential economic rivalries, rivalries which would persist just as vigorously if Britain and the U.S.A. were under a common government, rivalries which have indeed their exact counterpart within the U.S.A. in, for example, the conflicts between the textile manufacturers of New England and North Carolina. Admittedly the British and American interests involved seek and to some extent obtain in each country the potent backing of their government and admittedly the American Government's backing, if fully obtained, is potent indeed. But there are two limiting factors of which British opinion is seldom fully aware and for which it is seldom sufficiently grateful. The first is that although any individual American interest group may be very clamant for a one-way socialism (i.e. government benefits without government control), the American electorate at large is in many ways more suspicious of a government-directed economic drive than is the British; countervailing interest operates in the politico-economic, as well as in the purely economic realm. In addition to this there is another, and where Britain is concerned a more decisive, factor in

American policy throughout the post-war years; this is the pre-dominance, taken all in all, of political over merely economic considerations, or, to put it in other words, of the long over the short-term. Despite the concessions that have had to be made, to congressional or electoral pressure, or out of consideration for soft spots in the body economic, the truly impressive feature of American policy as it has finally emerged is the regard it has shown for certain persisting principles. Where Britain is involved these may be summed up as respect for her position as banker for the sterling area, concern to restore the viability of her economy and her balance of payments, determination to secure in Europe and the North Atlantic region in particular the largest practicable area of free exchange, and finally, with increasing emphasis as the earlier objectives have approached realization, a resolve to accelerate the development of backward areas in Asia, Africa and Latin America. That all these urges had a common spring in American self-interest is neither here nor there. What mattered to British policy-holders was that these American policies took due notice of British interests too and aimed at the creation and maintenance of an international economic order within which Britain could thrive. Arrived at by processes of open discussion in which not only official spokesmen but also the free play of economic argument and inquiry on both sides of the Atlantic played its part, they were proportionately reliable and stable despite all the buffeting of particular interests. As such, they formed a set of standards, mutually agreed, in relation to which British policy could, with some assurance, be shaped and to which, in the event of transatlantic disagreement, effective appeal could be made.

12

THE PARTNERSHIP

TO look back over the nexus of relationships which Britain maintains with the United States around the globe and in all sectors of national policy is to see that they fall, very roughly, into two categories. The first are mainly non-military, but are otherwise as diverse as the world-wide ramifications of British policy itself. They reflect often a rivalry but much more often a community of interests, public and private, which proceed from the past history and present interaction of our two societies. As such they do not lend themselves to any simple classification or exhaustive cataloguing. Though they have become both more extensive and intensive since 1938 they existed already—almost all of them—in the pre-war world and so served as the soil from which the peculiar intimacy of the wartime alliance took such quick and easy nourishment.

Since the war, however, the swiftly mounting challenge of the Communist states, particularly of the U.S.S.R., has drawn Britain and the U.S.A. together in a new defensive relationship which, though harmonizing readily enough (in the main) with the other, is different in character and aims. Its most oviously different characteristic is its extension to embrace a diversity of other anti-Communist powers, both in Europe and elsewhere; its typical vehicle is the multi-national alliance—N.A.T.O., C.E.N.T.O., S.E.A.T.O. If, within such alliances, the Anglo-American relationship is of peculiar importance, this is partly the consequence of their intimacy in the other sphere, partly the proportionate reflection of the scale of British, and Commonwealth, operations around the globe.

If very little has been said about this relationship in its most central aspect, as it bears directly on British policy towards the U.S.S.R., this is solely because here at any rate is a feature of the Anglo-American relationship so obvious as not to need stressing. No one can doubt for a moment that London's confrontation of Moscow rests on the assured and indispensable basis of Washington's support. Take that away and nothing remains. To say this, of course, is not to say that British policy "takes its orders" in this essential from Washington, but simply that both Britain and America recognize, like their common partners in the North Atlantic alliance, that a common front to Soviet pressure is the indispensable condition of their survival in freedom. But just as this fact is so obvious as hardly to need mention, so any elaboration of it (at least in the present, inevitable condition of official secrecy over the details of allied co-ordination) runs the grave risk of obscuring the substance of agreement by the accidents of controversy. It would not be difficult to chart any phase in the triangular relations of London, Washington and Moscow in terms of fairly well publicized Anglo-American disagreements about the precise timing, tactics or style of their approaches to the Kremlin. From Churchill's Fulton speech down to the negotiations over Berlin there have been differences, frankly acknowledged and openly aired, about how best to deal with the Russians. Nor in this continuing diplomatic conversation between the English-speaking capitals can either side claim to have had the last word. Now one, now the other, view has prevailed. Moreover, where so much of the disagreement has been tactical, very little of it can be ascribed consistently to an "American" or to a "British line". For these reasons a detailed analysis, even if practicable, is hardly profitable. There are, however, perhaps two differences in basic British and American attitudes here which are sufficiently sustained and important to merit a mention.

The first proceeds directly from geography and recent experience. Britain knows herself, by reason of size and accessibility, to be more directly vulnerable to destruction in any future war with the U.S.S.R. than the U.S.A. would be. She also knows, at first hand as a result of her experiences in 1940 and after, what aerial attack can do to a highly urban and centralized society. Consequently she has no illusions about the possibility of surviving a war waged with nuclear weapons. I am not aware that this has ever led her to indulge in appeasement of Soviet appetites or to contemplate the surrender of any agreed Anglo-American interest. But it has given her a more continuously vivid awareness of what a resort to war implies and provided a sharper, more urgent edge to her desires for a negotiated settlement. This, at least, in comparison with the attitudes publicly expressed by Americans at various levels below the very highest peaks of authority; it is at least arguable that when it comes to the conclusions reached by the ultimate decision makers in London and Washington there has been much less to choose than the publics of each country have sometimes assumed.

The second difference springs as much from national temperament and tradition as from specific experience; Americans lay greater stress on Communism *per se* as the enemy, Britons worry less about the ideology and show a greater readiness to accept the *faits accomplis* of Communist régimes. Manifestations of this occur at least as far back as the October Revolution. Britain recognized the Russian Communist régime in 1924, the U.S.A. not until 1933. The war intensified the contrast; Russia, as a result of Hitler's aggression, became an effective war ally in June, 1941, when the U.S.A. was still nominally at peace; the Anglo-Russian Treaty of May, 1942, never had any American counterpart. Yet, as we have seen, when the war ended the real distance between Washington and Moscow was no greater than that between London and Moscow and it was, in fact, a British leader who sounded the tocsin at Fulton, Missouri, in March, 1946. There *were* innate American and Russian affinities, as many observers, from Tocqueville onwards, have amply demonstrated. But they did not develop. Their place was taken, for obvious reasons, by a persistent rivalry and also, for less obvious reasons whose analysis lies beyond our scope, by a feeling of moral revulsion and often total detestation. The result was to give to American policy, where Russia was concerned, the air of a moral crusade. This note was seldom struck in Britain, where emphasis fell more often on the Russian-ness of the U.S.S.R.'s foreign policy, on its continuity with Tsarist imperialism, on its traditionalist obsessions with "warm water" or with the German menace or the Levant or Persia. Similarly with the satellites of Eastern Europe; the British were readier to accept their Communist governments as a distasteful but apparently unavoidable *cordon sanitaire* between the U.S.S.R. and the West, and were less reluctant to grant them official recognition and even to do business, commercial and cultural, even if not ideological, with puppet administrations which they despised but which they saw no way to remove short of all-out war. The Americans more obviously chafed at having to accept the blatant violations of solemn Soviet undertakings and of every human right which these régimes represented and made little or no attempt to find a *modus vivendi* with the worst of them.

It would be easy to document, by chapter and verse, these divergencies of national attitude to European Communism, and it would be idle to deny that official policies, in each country, owed something to the different temperatures of popular feeling which these attitudes generated. Yet if regard be paid solely to what was done by the governments of Britain and the U.S.A., ignoring what was so profusely said, the ensuing discrepancies will be found to be comparatively minor. Even under the most explicit apologist for the moral line, John Foster Dulles, it is doubtful whether the substance of American policy towards the U.S.S.R. was significantly different from that of Britain. Admittedly Dulles's weight was thrown against a summit meeting, with the result that the Geneva encounters of 1955 did not take place until Britain's most vocal advocate of "summitry", Winston Churchill, had retired from office. Admittedly too, Dulles delayed the Camp David encounter between Mr. Khrushchev and President Eisenhower in the autumn of 1959 (though he had acquiesced in it before his resignation in April). But if regard be had to the subject matter of the negotiations rather than to the timing or the form of them it is demonstrable that at neither of these meetings, nor yet at the subsequent "summits" of Paris in 1960 and Vienna in 1961, was there any substantial disagreement between Britain and the United States on the terms which should be offered or accepted. Moreover such differences as there were owed little or nothing to any distinction between a crusading and a pragmatic approach. All the evidence suggests that when it came to the clinch, in each of these unhappy encounters, it was the real, not the rhetorical, interests of the West which President and Prime Minister resolutely defended and that there was no substantial difference in the interpretation which each negotiator put upon them. In any case, with the waning of McCarthyism in the United States, the sobering shocks of sputnik and the U-2 fiasco, less was heard of anti-Communist crusades even in Congress or on the hustings and with the arrival of the Kennedy administration realism, patience and caution seem to have emerged as the dominant notes of American anti-Communism. There was thus perhaps in 1962 less divergence, in style or substance, between the Russian policies of Britain and the U.S.A. than at any time since the creation of N.A.T.O. in 1948–9.

Yet this, paradoxically, co-existed with a considerably lowered

169

vitality in N.A.T.O. itself. For that there were many reasons, some of which have been touched on earlier, but it would be dishonest not to recognize that the working of the Anglo-American partnership was one of them.[1] We have noted the contradiction that was built into N.A.T.O. at its very inception, that though a multi-nation alliance in form, its essential strength was derived from the possession by one member of a deterrent denied to the rest and uncontrolled by them. So long, however, as the U.S.A. also made its full contribution in conventional forces this constituted no weakness in the alliance—was indeed an extra source of strength. It was when the doctrine of "massive retaliation" with non-consultative overtones was advertised that the problems created by the nuclear deterrent began to corrode the alliance. When Britain, by unaided efforts, broke the American monopoly of the deterrent and developed subsequently its own variant of reliance on the nuclear weapon solidarity was further impaired. The French acquisition of an atomic bomb took the process of disintegration a step further.

The British deterrent, though independently obtained, admitted her, as we have seen, to a sharing of American atomic secrets. This was mistakenly understood, amongst many members of N.A.T.O., conspicuously France, as constituting the basis of the distinctive Anglo-American partnership; as such it stimulated the demand for each member to have his own deterrent and so to gain admission to the "atomic club", or else for the creation of a N.A.T.O. deterrent, whatever exactly that might mean. But although certain admitted benefits did accrue to Britain in her relations with the U.S.A. from the possession of a deterrent of her own, it was not from this that the "special relationship" (if indeed it was "special") derived its speciality. It did not even derive it from the partnership which preceded the British deterrent—the availability of Britain as the unsinkable aircraft carrier for S.A.C. Valuable as this was for American strategy, this was not a unique service which Britain rendered; other S.A.C. bases were soon established in Europe, Asia and Africa in countries none of which acquired thereby a larger voice in the alliance. What then was the essential nature of Britain's relationship with the U.S.A. during these years and from what did it derive?

[1] Though paradoxically it was also the axis around which the rest of NATO largely revolved.

There was one thing which it was not; it was not a treaty relationship. The only important treaty relationships which Britain has or has had with the U.S.A. since the war are the familiar anti-Communist, multilateral ones of which N.A.T.O. is both the prototype and the most successful example. There are indeed bilateral agreements in plenty[1] and some of these admit Britain to a preferred, exclusive defence relationship, mainly those relating to atomic energy. But even the most cherished—or envied—of these cannot be said to be the basis on which rests the close understanding between London and Washington. They are the results, not the causes, of that understanding. And not surprisingly, therefore, the intimate consultation which is the best expression of that understanding does not proceed through the channels established by any of these written undertakings, not even those of N.A.T.O. itself. To go back to the distinction made at the beginning of this chapter, any especial intimacy which Britain and the U.S.A. maintain in their anti-Communist operations and organizations derives essentially from a community of interests which is both logically and chronologically prior to it.[2]

More surprising perhaps than the reluctance to codify the relationship in a treaty is the stubborn refusal to incorporate, or even symbolize, it in an institution. The United States may not be a country of very strong institutional growths, but Britain is, in almost all departments of its national life. Yet there is no Anglo-American equivalent of the Commonwealth Prime Ministers' Conference, or even of that shadowy wraith, the Council of Europe. There are indeed Anglo-American institutions a-plenty, but they are all private associations, smiled on sometimes by governments, patronized by officials, but never claiming to represent legislatures

[1] A list of them is provided in Appendix A.

[2] Although at a thousand points co-operation in the North Atlantic and other alliances has intensified that community of interests, in one important sense it has actually proved an embarrassment for it. As loyal allies with the rest, both Britain and the United States have repeatedly had to disavow in public an intimacy which they enjoy in private. Indeed their characteristic posture is often that of the laconic heroes of Victorian boys' fiction whose amity is best expressed in a silent hand-clasp and averted gaze, with perhaps only the occasional tribute, at a Pilgrims, or English-Speaking Union dinner, of a tear dashed away from a manly blushing cheek.

or executives on either side of the Atlantic. The nearest both sides
have ever come to creating such an embodiment of their relationship is in the recurrent meetings of President and Prime Minister,
first instituted by Roosevelt and Churchill in the war, then largely
intermitted by Truman and Attlee, but subsequently resumed with
an increasing frequency.[1] However, important as these encounters
are, they are not by any means distinctive or exclusively Anglo-
American; they are only the application to that relationship of a
diplomatic technique which the aeroplane has made possible and,
because possible, obligatory for heads of state everywhere. Though
by their frequency or otherwise they provide a rough indication of
the intimacy of consultation at the highest levels between London
and Washington, it is a very rough indication indeed. If we had a
chart of the telephone calls between Number Ten and the White
House that would tell us a good deal more.

The fact is that the distinctive feature of the Anglo-American
relationship, so far as governments are concerned, exists at a much
more mundane level. It is to be found in the generally informal,
frequently unofficial co-operation that has grown up as a kind of
second nature between civil servants and diplomats on each side of
the Atlantic, based on an experience of mutual trust and a joint
pragmatic approach to common problems, the whole over-arched
by a sense of common interests and common values—and, of course,
enormously facilitated by the use of a common language. In
London and Washington—and indeed in many other capitals where
British and American officials find themselves working together—
this often finds expression in committee meetings at a departmental
level which provide for regular consultation and discussion over a
wide range of matters of common concern. However even in these
it is not necessarily in the formal confrontation over minutes and
agenda papers that the relationship has its most distinctive expression. A seasoned American observer has given his impression
of what this means where defence is concerned:

"There are dozens of long, vehement, good-natured talks
between diplomats and soldiers, airmen and sailors here, in
Washington and elsewhere. Each participant carries into such
discussions all his national prejudices. But each is also conscious

[1] See Appendix B for a list of such meetings to date.

172

THE PARTNERSHIP

of the over-riding problem of winning the long duel with the U.S.S.R. to the extent that, in the small hours, the two nationalities often merge into a common effort."[1]

What Mr. Middleton says about the diplomats and fighting men could equally well be applied to the economists and administrators. The working relationships thus established not only guarantee a smooth discharge of decisions arrived at at the highest levels; they reflect and create a climate of common purpose and frank discussion. Consequently they persist, by a healthy momentum of their own, even when, as at Suez, rupture and conflict impair the functioning of "the highest levels". There is thus a kind of Anglo-American Gulf Stream whose flow is little affected by the tempests which may disturb the Atlantic surface.

To say this is not to ignore certain evident differences in the British and American ways of doing business which show up in the deliberations of officials no less than in the encounters of private persons. The government which the British official represents is comparatively small, trim and tidy, close-knit in its operations, internally fairly disciplined and co-operative, equally seasoned in all its important parts and generally stable both in its internal composition and in its relationship to parliament and the country. The American executive by contrast is large, loose, even sprawling, set by the Constitution and still more by the facts of the society it serves under the jurisdiction of two masters, the President and Congress, fluid in its individual membership[2] and fluctuating in its popular support. The one enjoys privacy, the other lives always on the frontier of publicity. Hardly surprising therefore if the combined functioning of two such entities, or of their representatives, gives rise to a sufficiency of those frictions, flurries, leaks, dropped catches, or missed goals which form the frequent gossip of the official capitals and supply much of the material for newspapers. The most obvious operational weaknesses are likely, for the reasons listed above, to be on the American side, and to be most amply documented in Washington. It is, however, worth remembering

[1] Drew Middleton in *New York Times*, 25 February, 1960.

[2] As Mr. James Reston once pointed out, "the Department of State has been in a constant state of reorganization ever since World War II": *New York Times*, 20 November, 1956.

that in such a relationship the too smooth functioning of a too professional team may carry hazards of its own as great as the uncoordinated "playing by ear" of the amateurs. What is elegant and intellectually satisfying in Whitehall may wear quite another appearance in Washington; in a fast-changing world there are no absolute experts, in administration or anything else, and the American contribution often gains a creative edge from its very unprofessionalism. Moreover, unified as the Whitehall team may be, it seldom plays alone; the Commonwealth partners, whose significance has been earlier remarked, sometimes complicate life for American negotiators who are accustomed to seeing such relationships in the comparatively orderly form of the federal structure. To find, as the leader of an alliance, exactly when to speak and what to say to all the members of the Commonwealth on the matter of a developing negotiation which concerns them all, but not all equally—that is as pretty a problem for the American diplomat as any that the American separation of powers creates for the British. For Britain too, as her maternal authority wanes in a world where parents are not what they used to be, there are problems whenever she has to negotiate with the United States on matters that affect other members of the Commonwealth as well as herself. Even the "Canadian bridge", valuable as it often is, can sometimes become a "clover-leaf" on which the traffic has got into the wrong lanes.[1]

[1] It is much to be regretted that we have so little record of what the Anglo-American partnership is like at this working level. One of the few accounts of it written from within is that provided by Sir Erich Roll in *The Combined Food Board*, Stanford, 1956. He sums up his impressions as follows (p. 306):

"Some commentators have stressed the effectiveness of the British, Combined Board team and have compared it favourably with that of the American. It is true that more of the initiative came from the British side and that with much smaller numbers the British were able at the least to equal the American contribution. But this is hardly surprising. Here was a small, compact team, having at its disposal an amalgam of different qualities which a picked staff of varied antecedents was able to contribute, depending upon a highly refined and efficient machine at home, never in doubt either as to its broad objectives or as to the limits of its discretion on immediate issues, having undivided responsibility over the entire field and, above all, because of the general character of combined machinery in Washington, exerting considerable influence in the councils at home. It would have been

For these and for other reasons this crucial "middle level" co-operation in the Anglo-American field is no automatic, self-regulating mechanism. It requires all the skill and devotion which its practitioners can bring to it and all the guidance and stimulus which are provided by the wider, extra-governmental Anglo-American community of which it is merely a partial expression.

---

astonishing, indeed, if in these circumstances it had not acquitted itself well. What is far more remarkable is the speed with which the American members, many of whom were necessarily less experienced in these matters, were able, whenever the basic issue of their relations to national responsibility and power was successfully resolved, to operate with ease and assurance. It is true that there were some "tricks of the trade" in combined procedure, such as methods of preparing meetings and papers, co-ordination of instructions, effective liaison inside and out, and all the other paraphernalia of smooth administration in which the British were more at home. But there too the Americans quickly learned; and on the major question of processing issues for decision, there was not, in the outcome, any particular advantage on the British side.

"The British may claim to have helped improve the United States machinery at least by example, though sometimes by the kind of direct precept which is permissible among friends and allies—an achievement which is by no means diminished by the fact that it was based on a sort of enlightened self-interest. The British soon learned that their main concern was not in gaining some quick short-term advantage, but rather that lasting benefit to themselves (and to the common cause) depended upon the effectiveness of the combined machine and thus upon the effectiveness, day in, day out, of the United States machine. Clarification and, where appropriate concentration of responsibility of the American side, even if it tended in the short run to militate against some desirable United Kingdom objective, was in itself desirable, since it would be bound to lead to more effective co-operation in the long run.

"In all this the Canadians played an extremely useful part. Being fortunate in possessing a governmental machine which seemed to combine the best features of the British with the best of the American, closely tied politically and economically (in food particularly) to the United Kingdom, yet having powerful bonds also with the United States and being often faced with very similar domestic repercussions of international decisions, they were able to make most valuable, and at times, decisive, contributions to finding solutions that were acceptable to all . . ."

175

Fortunately for its good health, the part it expresses is quite a good deal of the whole, as the common concerns of British and American governments have come to range far beyond the traditional province of diplomacy. An eloquent symbol of this is provided by the British Embassy in Washington which has added to the country house elegance of the original Lutyens building a far larger, frankly utilitarian Chancery block which handles the day-to-day office work of a microcosm of Whitehall. Behind this brick and glass façade almost 600 persons, the largest embassy staff in Washington, are engaged not primarily in "representation" as it was once known, nor yet in "negotiation", but in the task of maintaining contact with their American opposite numbers over what is virtually the entire field of British government—from agriculture to the West Indies. In London an even larger (and considerably more elegant) structure in Grosvenor Square houses an equivalent range of American officials discharging a similar function in relation to their opposite numbers. What the activities of these practitioners are helping to create is hardly indeed, in the conventional sense of the term, an alliance at all; it is more nearly a community.

Viewed from London, in 1945 or 1946, this community or alliance had two principal functions to discharge. The first was to provide American aid in restoring Britain's war-crippled economy and in reconstructing a ruined Europe. The second was to prevent any return to American isolationism and to guarantee that American power would be mobilized to check Russian expansionism. Looking back over the fifteen years that followed, it is evident that both objectives have been realized. Thanks in part to the Financial Agreements of 1946, but more more to the European Recovery and Mutual Aid Programmes, the United Kingdom and Western Europe both found themselves enjoying a higher degree of prosperity than they had ever known, with economies resting on far more stable foundations than in 1938. Thanks largely to the first Truman administration and contemporary Republican leadership in the Senate, American isolationism was routed and by successive stands, over Greece and Turkey, over Berlin, over the North Atlantic Treaty, over Korea, the balance of power in Europe, and largely in the world outside, was held. In the process of so doing a new relationship had developed between Britain and the United States. Though the U.S.A. had assumed many of the global defence burdens which had previously been Britain's, it was no longer a relationship merely of British dependence upon American strength. There was also an American recognition of her need for an ally who maintained some structure of order in a generally chaotic world and could even assist in the defence of the United States. In the pre-sputnik era she had helped to keep America's frontier on the further side of the Atlantic; in the post-sputnik era of over-leaped frontiers she could still house weapons of deterrence that lost their efficacy if housed in America itself.

But as the racing minute hand of invention passed from A-bomb, through H-bomb, to I.C.B.M., the conviction intensified in London and in Washington that the protection afforded by the new weapons was fragile indeed. They were a sword hardly less perilous to wield than to be smitten by. The result was a fresh search for some point of *détente* with the Soviets and, if possible, some agreed and controlled disarmament. Britain and the U.S.A. had their differences of tempo and technique over this, which did not frustrate (even though they sometimes obscured) the parallelism of their approaches. A great deal of diplomatic history of the late fifties is made up of the details of abortive Anglo-American negotiations with the Russians, but for any student of the alliance two points stand out. The first, that the Russians never got anywhere in their endeavours to divide Britain and America; the second, that Britain and America never got very far in their search for a settlement. At most they only learnt to live with their problem and hoped it would be willing to live with them.

Similarly in the economic field the relationship between the United Kingdom and the United States had moved away from the simple dependence of poor debtor on rich creditor. The huge discrepancy of wealth and resources remained, but Britain now stood reasonably firmly on her own feet, capable of being an active partner, not a mere protegé, in the tasks of economic leadership that the Atlantic Alliance had to undertake around the world. Meanwhile a Western Europe, revitalized in large part by American (and indeed British) efforts, had emerged as a new bastion of economic, and so potentially of political, strength. Whether the European Economic Community developed as a "third Force" or as a counterbalancing but still integrated element in the Atlantic Alliance depended on the relationship which first Britain and then the U.S.A. succeeded in establishing with it. To the simple concept of "integrating Europe" was now being added in the U.S.A. a new and sophisticated awareness of the need to prevent any new European economic block from being exclusive and restrictionist. By machinery such as O.E.C.D., by the strengthening of international agencies such as G.A.T.T. and the Fund, and by moves in the direction of a freer American trading policy, it was hoped to guarantee that the economic energies of the new Europe would be outward-flowing throughout the Atlantic area and beyond. Britain, forced at last to contemplate a plunge which created major problems for her domestic economy, for her Commonwealth relations and for her associations with the United States, was bound to welcome an American interest which promised active participation in the venture. There was at last a good prospect that if Britain went in with the Six she would not be committed to an association which would weaken historic and essential transatlantic links.

Meanwhile, however, beyond the European and North Atlantic areas, a new world had grown up, as different in many ways from the world of 1945 as from the world of 1938. Its dynamism was variously labelled as "anti-colonialism", "anti-Western nationalism" or "the revolution of rising expectations", though none of these appelations fully described its character. Two things, however, were certain about it—that it gave to aggressive Communism a new weapon against the West with which to overleap the N.A.T.O., C.E.N.T.O. and S.E.A.T.O. walls, and also that the problems it presented were not such as could be solved by any simple resort to force, as in Suez, or by mere metropolitanism, as in Algeria, or by mere aid, as in Laos. As far as Britain was concerned, moreover, though she had won important interim successes in some areas, like South-East Asia or West Africa, it was apparent that neither here nor elsewhere, as in the Middle East, could she— or the Commonwealth—provide single-handed a solution that gave any promise of permanence. And with every year of the fifties that passed the number of countries so affected and the degree of their affection increased.

It cannot be said that the alliance displayed the same vitality, unity and creativeness in meeting this challenge as it had in the great days between 1947 and 1950 which saved Western Europe. Suez, in a sense, was the classic expression of its inadequacy. In the light of that disaster, however, a growing awareness had developed in Britain and America of the shape and dimensions of the task before them. The Eisenhower-Macmillan meeting of October,

1957, and the N.A.T.O. meeting which followed it gave much currency to the concept of "interdependence". "The countries of the free world are interdependent and only in genuine partnership, by combining their resources and sharing tasks in many fields, can progress and safety be found."[1] At the time and in the light of the actions immediately taken this was primarily understood as referring to the numbers of the Anglo-American alliance and beyond them to all the members of N.A.T.O. But it soon became apparent that the words were susceptible of a wider meaning—and that in fact they needed to be so interpreted if the essential interests, perhaps of any members, but certainly of Britain and the U.S.A., were to be safeguarded. In a shrinking world (and an expanding U.N.) the fortunes and preferences of the so-called "underdevelopeds" were daily acquiring a new significance; a Northern hemispheric partnership which left out of account the emerging South would soon find itself stalled in the animosity of the poor and the wreckage of its own most essential values. Of course, neither in Britain nor elsewhere had this challenge gone wholly by default; it was part, at least, of the historic mission of the Commonwealth. But the fifties provoked an acceleration of pressures so great as to constitute a virtually new challenge and one which neither Britain nor anyone else could meet alone. It involved both the elimination of the last stigma of inferiority that attached to colonialism and the extension to other parts of the world of the benefits of Western technology. Britain, with the legacy of the greatest imperial power, and the United States, as creator and manager of the greatest productive machine in history, had irresistible commitments here. They laboured also under painful disabilities—a tenacious tradition of colour prejudice in both societies, an adherence in Britain, often in unexpected quarters, to outmoded attitudes and incompatible interests, the prevalence in America of *simpliste* approaches, political or administrative, to situations of historic complexity. But they also enjoyed certain assets derived from their history and the nature of their society. Their democratic and liberal traditions offered the best guarantees available to human fraility that they would subordinate sectional interests to a wider view and learn some at least of the lessons of experience. The United States had resources, inventiveness, generosity and *élan*; Britain had the partnership of the

[1] Communiqué of the Eisenhower-Macmillan meetings, 25 October, 1957.

Commonwealth and a tradition of administrative pragmatism. In combination, these assets and these attitudes offered a fair chance that the size of the problem would be realized and a serious effort would be made to find a solution. It could not be an exclusively Anglo-American solution. It would require the co-operation of Europe, the mediation of international agencies, the admission even of the clients to an equality with their patrons. But without the partnership of Britain and America it was fairly certain that no peaceful solution would be found.

APPENDIX A

Principal Treaties and Agreements between the British and United States Governments, June, 1945 to December, 1960

(References are to the Treaty Series and to Command Papers, HMG = Her Majesty's Government and USG = Government of the U.S.A.)

T.S. No. 17 (1946)
Cmd. 6837

Agreements between the Governments represented at the Bermuda Telecommunications Conference. Bermuda, 4 Dec., 1945.

T.S. No. 53 (1946)
Cmd. 6968

Financial Agreements between HMG and USG. Washington, 6 Dec., 1945.

T.S. No. 3 (1946)
Cmd. 6747

Final Act of the Aviation Conference and Agreements between HMG and USG relating to Air Services. Bermuda, 11 Feb., 1946.

T.S. No. 13 (1946)
Cmd. 6813

Settlement for Lend-Lease, Reciprocal Aid, Surplus War Property and Claims. Washington, 27 March, 1946.

T.S. No. 41 (1948)
Cmd. 7469

Economic Co-operation Agreement between HMG and USG. London, 6 July, 1948.

T.S. No. 69 (1948)
Cmd. 7527

Agreement for the Establishment of the U.S. Educational Commission [so-called Fulbright Commission] in the U.K. London, 22 Sept., 1948.

T.S. No. 56 (1949)
Cmd. 7789

North Atlantic Treaty. Washington, 4 April, 1949

T.S. No. 13 (1950)
Cmd. 7894

Mutual Defence Assistance Agreement. Washington, 27 Jan., 1950.

T.S. No. 74 (1950)
Cmnd. 8109

Agreement for the Establishment in the Bahama Islands of a Proving-Ground for Guided Missiles. Washington, 21 July, 1950.

181

(Extended to cover additional sites by further agreements on 15 Jan., 1952, 25 June, 1956 and 1 April, 1957.)

T.S. No. 3 (1955)
Cmnd. 9363 — Status of Forces Agreement of Parties to the North Atlantic Treaty. London, June 19, 1951.

T.S. No. 9 (1953)
Cmd. 8757 — Agreement to Facilitate the Interchange of Patents and Technical Information for Defence Purposes. London, 19 Jan., 1953.

T.S. No. 63 (1957)
Cmnd. 265 — The South-East Asia Collective Defence Treaty. Manila, Sept. 8, 1954.

T.S. No. 52 (1955)
Cmnd. 9555 — Agreement for Co-operation regarding Atomic Information for Mutual Defence Purposes. Washington, 15 June, 1955.

T.S. No. 55 (1955)
Cmnd. 9560 — Agreement for Co-operation on the Peaceful Uses of Atomic Energy. Washington, 15 June, 1955.

T.S. No. 44 (1957)
Cmnd. 178 — Agreement amending the Financial Agreements of Dec. 6, 1945 (The "Waiver"). Washington, March 6, 1957.

T.S. No. 14 (1958)
Cmnd. 406 — Exchange of Notes Concerning the Supply to the U.K. Government of I.R.B.Ms. Washington, 22 Feb., 1958.

T.S. No. 41 (1958)
Cmnd. 537 — Agreement for Co-operation on the Uses of Atomic Energy for Mutual Defence Purposes. Washington, 3 July, 1958. (amended on 7 May, 1959).

T.S. No. 24 (1960)
Cmnd. 1034 — Exchange of Notes ... Setting up of a Ballistic Missile Early Warning Station in the U.K. London, 15 February, 1960.

APPENDIX B

Meetings of British Prime Ministers and United States Presidents since World War II

1945	Nov. 10–16	Attlee—Truman	at Washington
1950	Dec. 4–9	Attlee—Truman	at Washington
1952	Jan. 5–22	Churchill—Truman	at Washington
1953	Jan. 5–8	Churchill—Eisenhower	at Washington
	Dec. 4–7	Churchill—Eisenhower—Laniel	at Bermuda
1954	June 25–28	Churchill—Eisenhower	at Washington
1955	July 17–23	Eden—Eisenhower—Faure —Bulganin (Summit Meeting)	at Geneva
1956	Jan 30–Feb. 3	Eden—Eisenhower	at Washington
1957	Mar. 21–24	Macmillan—Eisenhower	at Bermuda
	Oct. 23–25	Macmillan—Eisenhower	at Washington
	Dec. 16–19	Macmillan—Eisenhower etc. (N.A.T.O. Heads of Government)	at Paris
1958	June 7–11	Macmillan—Eisenhower	at Washington
1959	Mar. 19–23	Macmillan—Eisenhower	at Washington
	Aug. 27–Sept. 2	Eisenhower—Macmillan	at London
1960	Mar. 27–29	Macmillan—Eisenhower	at Washington
	Sept. 27	Macmillan—Eisenhower	at U.N.
1961	Mar. 26	Macmillan—Kennedy	at Key West
	April 4–9	Macmillan—Kennedy	at Washington
	June 4–5	Kennedy—Macmillan	at London
	Dec. 12–22	Macmillan—Kennedy	at Bermuda
1962	April 28–29	Macmillan—Kennedy	at Washington

APPENDIX C

British Ambassadors to the United States

Sir Ronald Lindsay	appointed	11 May, 1930
The Marquis of Lothian	,,	29 Aug., 1939
Viscount Halifax	,,	22 Dec., 1940
Lord Inverchapel	,,	25 Jan., 1946
/ Sir Oliver Franks	,,	22 May, 1948
Sir Roger Makins	,,	31 Dec., 1952
\ Sir Harold Caccia	,,	2 Nov., 1956
Sir David Ormsby-Gore	,,	21 May, 1961

American Ambassadors to the United Kingdom

Mr. Joseph P. Kennedy	,,	7 Jan., 1938
Mr. John G. Winant	,,	6 Feb., 1941
/ Mr. W. Averell Harriman	,,	23 Mar., 1946
Mr. Lewis W. Douglas	,,	26 Feb., 1947
Mr. Walter S. Gifford	,,	7 Dec., 1950
Mr. Winthrop W. Aldrich	,,	2 Feb., 1953
Mr. John Hay Whitney	,,	7 Feb., 1957
' Mr. David K. E. Bruce	,,	2 Feb., 1961

INDEX

INDEX

INDEX